TRANSNATIONAL BUSINESS AND CORPORATE CULTURE

PROBLEMS AND OPPORTUNITIES

edited by

STUART BRUCHEY
ALLAN NEVINS PROFESSOR EMERITUS
COLUMBIA UNIVERSITY

T0303950

TRANSNATIONAL MARKETING IN THE INFORMATION AGE

DIANE DESIMONE

NEW YORK AND LONDON

First published 1998 by Garland Publishing, Inc.

This edition published 2013 by Routledge
711 Third Avenue, New York, NY 10017, USA
2 Park Square, Milton Park, Abingdon, Oxfordshire OX14 4RN

First issued in paperback 2016

Routledge is an imprint of the Taylor & Francis Group, an informa business

Library of Congress Cataloging-in-Publication Data

DeSimone, Diane, 1949–
    Transnational marketing in the information age / Diane
DeSimone.
        p.   cm. — (Transnational business and corporate
culture)
    Includes bibliographical references and index.
    ISBN 0-8153-3311-0 (alk. paper)
    1. Export marketing. 2. International business enterprises.
I. Title. II. Series.
HF1416.D47 1998
658.8'48—dc21
                                                                98-42965

ISBN 13: 978-1-138-98606-0 (pbk)
ISBN 13: 978-0-8153-3311-1 (hbk)

This work is dedicated to my husband, mother, and sister who have always supported my efforts in any undertaking; to the professional marketers around the world striving to understand the values of their global customers; and especially to Mr. Jim Nelson who loved contemplative thought, challenging issues and intellectual conversation on any subject; who touched so many lives from his quiet place on the Eastern Shore, and who was a special friend and mentor to me.

Contents

Preface

Today's rapidly expanding global business environment, fueled by the exponential advancements in information communications technologies, has created a need for change in traditional marketing theory. The new technologies not only allow but compel businesses of all sizes to compete in the global marketplace. Consequently, the new questions of transnational, multi-cultural marketing utilizing advanced technologies add entirely new facets to the basic marketing issues of product, price, promotion, and distribution.

This work began with the recognition of a discontinuity in current corporate marketing. When questioned as to whether they study a culture and try to assimilate cultural needs into products and promotions being offered in foreign countries, corporations always responded positively. However, people outside the corporate environment indicated otherwise. It seemed as if companies would visit a new country to assess a market, notice that many people were wearing "yellow", and then assume that products needed to be "yellow". Of course, corporations did not take new markets quite that lightly; however, there was an obvious lack of in depth understanding of the cultural value set and its origins within the people in the new target markets. Thus, the information presented here discusses the need for true transnational marketing, and presents an example of what that may entail.

The first section presented in this book describes the needed changes to the traditional core marketing issues in order to address the new transnational environment. It also describes the critical requirements of understanding the cultural core values of new markets, and incorporating the knowledge of these values in marketing strategies. By addressing the traditional theories, and offering a critical comparison to the proposed enhancements for transnational marketing, the section prepares the reader for the development of a marketing strategy in the second section.

The second section utilizes a scenario to demonstrate the application of the enhanced marketing techniques. This scenario depicts in story form the development of a marketing strategy for the introduction of a business to business product into Mexico. Besides demonstrating the traditional issues of global marketing, the scenario also includes the elements of political economics and sociological culture that a transnational marketer must take into consideration when implementing a marketing strategy in a new country market. It does not purport to provide all the answers to the questions that arise in the development of a transnational marketing strategy; but is intended to raise the issues and the sensitivity of the marketers in order that they may know to seek out the information pertinent to their own strategy and situation. The techniques and resources described in the scenario can be applied to whichever new markets companies plan to enter.

Introduction

The information provided in this book is intended to serve as a practical guide to those venturing into transnational business. It is not intended to be a restatement of already written, excellent information on the means of developing international markets. However, with the rapid changes in today's commercial environment, borders are becoming nearly transparent in many ways. Free trade agreements and unions are decreasing or eliminating the barriers to commerce between member countries. Technologies are creating nearly instantaneous, world-wide information flows. Corporate mergers and alliances are blurring the national boundaries of individual companies. These accelerating changes are, in turn, changing the environment and requirements for international marketing.

In marketing, although the basic issues around product, price, promotion, and distribution will still be core issues to be dealt with, the additional questions of transnational, multi-cultural marketing utilizing rapidly advancing information communication technologies add entirely new facets to those core issues. The new millennium will continue to broaden the perspective of those issues.

Additionally, although many corporations today try to observe different customs of countries in which they are marketing product and service, few if any actually study the cultural values of the different countries. As more and more companies are capable of marketing internationally through the communications technologies, and competition becomes more demanding, the need for recognizing, appreciating, and supporting a country's core values in the implementation of marketing strategies becomes critical to success. This book identifies the changes required in traditional marketing theory and the knowledge gaps that need to be filled as information communications technologies open the global marketplace and are applied to marketing strategies to shrink time and distance between companies and worldwide customers.

This book contains two distinct sections which the reader can address in either order. Section one will aid the reader in working through the second section; therefore it can be used a primer for the section two, or as a way to provide answers to questions section two generates.

The first section describes the needed changes to the traditional core marketing issues in order to address the new transnational environment. It reviews the potential for and the impact of the use of information communications technologies in marketing strategies. This section also considers the subject of cultural core values and the techniques for determining these values. It addresses the traditional theories, and offers a critical comparison to the proposed enhancements for transnational marketing.

The second section builds on the first by applying the learning regarding transnational marketing and the use of information communications technologies in the development of a marketing strategy to create the scenario. Marketers need to form a holistic view of the environment and begin to understand that altering one element of the marketing mix has ramifications for the whole strategy. This becomes even more critical when the situation is complicated by multiple cultures, economies, and distances as in a transnational market environment. Scenarios developed through the incorporation of the interdisciplinary research findings and real life examples can provide a realistic environment to allow marketers to try out a strategy and anticipate the results. By combining discoveries in the disciplines of technology, political economics, sociology, cultural anthropology, and marketing, a potential scenario has been developed that will present a marketer with probable situations occurring in transnational markets when information communications technologies are applied. Then, the marketer can use the text to explore the possible impacts on the once traditional marketing problems of product, price, promotion, and distribution. As different decisions are made, they will impact all aspects of the marketing situation which may, in turn, affect the overall environment. Changes in the environment alter the scenario and the whole problem changes and must be addressed again. Practicing the basic concepts in a scenario and predicting the consequences, good or bad, will ingrain the basics into the marketer's habits while demonstrating, at the same time, that there is no one right answer. As the situations evolve, the strategies and "answers" must evolve.

This scenario depicts the development of a marketing strategy for the introduction of a business to business product into Mexico. The scenario also includes the elements of political economics and sociological culture to be considered when a company begins implementing a marketing strategy in Mexico.

Although Mexico has been chosen to make the scenario specific and realistic, the process is applicable to other markets as well. The scenario format has been chosen in order to bring to life experiences and anecdotes that the reader might more easily remember. As marketers go through the strategy development process for their own products and services, recalling the story may be helpful to recalling things to do, sources to find, and potential mistakes to avoid.

This book does not purport to provide all the answers to the questions that arise in the development of a transnational marketing strategy. The intent here is to raise the issues and the sensitivity of the marketers in order that they may know to seek out the information pertinent to their own strategy and situation. The first step to avoiding or solving a problem is to ask the right questions.

Transnational Marketing in
the Information Age

Transnational Marketing—Concept

Is It Still the Product, Price, Promotion, & Place "Business as Usual" in a Transnational Market?

Why is international marketing of critical importance to the professional marketer of the 21st century? Simple, all of the trends in today's business world point to the need for companies of all sizes to engage in cross border, if not world wide, trade. In industrialized countries, home markets are saturated forcing companies to look to other countries to continue growth. At the same time, developing countries focus on external markets to gain an inflow of capital and revenue to support their requirements for building infrastructure and to supply the needs of their growing middle class. Consequently, companies that currently consider themselves in domestic markets will at the very least need to defend their home market from companies entering from other countries. More likely, companies will find themselves having to move into international markets themselves to support their own growth and to support their customers who are also increasingly becoming international.

Figure 1. The 4 "P's" of Marketing Strategy

In addition to supporting international customers, companies find themselves dealing more and more with international suppliers. The growing number of free trade unions force companies to reconsider their supply agreements. To remain cost competitive with quality products, companies will look at a much broader selection of resource, parts, and service suppliers when considering a new product development. An international marketing strategy must consider supply availability when making product decisions.

Further, marketing strategies are forced into considering international aspects based on the interdependence of world economics. A significant change in the exchange rate in one part of the world may suddenly cause the domestic market to be more or less attractive to foreign competition. Recessions and recoveries are generally world-wide swings with shorter lead times between geographic areas. A sudden shift in one of the major stock markets can quickly play havoc with the viability of a company's key customers, or with the company itself.

All of these trends are complicated and accelerated even more by the exponential growth in information communications technologies. Via communications, events in one part of the world immediately impact markets in other parts. Sophisticated customers and suppliers who are technologically advanced expect to be supported anywhere in the world with advanced systems from flexible promotion campaigns, to on-line order entry and status, to customized products. In many industries, marketing information systems have become key competitive differentiators.

NEW INFORMATION REQUIREMENTS

Thus, given that marketing in the 21st century will be international, what sort of new information will a marketer need beyond the requirements of a domestic strategy? To develop a marketing strategy for successful penetration into another country market, the marketer needs to actively seek information that is inherently "known" about one's own country. An understanding and appreciation of the culture, values, history, geography, laws, political environment, and future direction of the country are required in order to assess the impact each of these elements will have on the strategy.

The culture and underlying values indigenous to the people of a country are perhaps the most pervasive elements that will affect the results of a marketing plan, and yet, are the most difficult to truly understand. Culture is usually recognized as something the marketer must know; but little time and effort is given to the study of it. One theory, offered by Theodore Levitt in recent years, is that information communication technologies are homogenizing cultures anyway. This view, however, confuses customs with culture. "Customs borrowing" has always occurred when different peoples merge; and the communications technologies, especially television and radio, will accelerate this phenomenon. However, the core values of a people change very little, and play a more dominant role as the technologies cause cultures to interact on a daily basis. The core values and consequent culture can significantly alter the marketer's product, promotion, and price decisions based on what is permitted and valued.

Gaining an understanding of a country's culture is crucial, and a subsequent chapter will be devoted to this subject. At the moment, for the discussion of new information to be obtained, consider two elements of culture—language and religion. Cateora and Czinkota and Ronkainen, in their respective marketing texts, have emphasized the need for the marketer to learn the language of the new market. The value is not in just learning the words. Language is an expression of meaning beyond words. Understanding the expressions and nuances of a language helps one to develop an understanding of the things the people value. Note also, the words that do not exist in the language to be sensitive to the differences in the values of the predominantly

English speaking cultures compared to others. For example, in many Far Eastern languages the concept of individual personalities separate from the whole earth does not exist. Unity and oneness with the world is a core value. Language is a source of pride to a people; consequently, those interested in developing a long lasting relationship with a new country market will learn the language.

Studying the religious evolution of a country can provide deep insight into the values and culture of a people. History, traditions, beliefs, and even superstitions come together in the basic religious values of a people. The international marketer needs at least a high level understanding of the main religious beliefs and traditions in order to consider them when structuring business transactions, defining products, and developing promotional plans.

Language and religion are the two cultural elements that are the most visible and that change the least from generation to generation. These are the elements that people fight for. Products and marketing strategies that conflict with either of these cultural aspects will not succeed.

A country's history is information of equal importance to a marketer as the culture. As Cateora points out, history is typically fact mixed with perception, and one must understand that country's perception. For example, from the perspective of the United States, most Americans consider the Monroe Doctrine to be a means of protecting Mexico from being taken over by Europe. To many Mexicans, the history of the Monroe Doctrine is perceived as interference by the United States and a U.S. attempt at cultural dominance. Such perceptual differences can significantly impact marketing decisions. Consider how many product promotions in the Unites States base their appeal on glorifying World War II or the Wild West—neither of which would work well in Mexico.

Two important roles are played by a country's geography—often overlooked even in one's home country, not to mention a new country market. First, geography helps determine the customs, traditions, and activities of people in various regions. People who have grown up near the sea usually have traditions based on families of fishermen, while those from fertile inland areas have customs stemming from farming families and communities. People from cold weather climates will tend to have very different interests, customs, and tendencies than those from warm weather climates. Geert Hofstede has even attributed some differences in the core cultural aspects of risk avoidance and individualism to the climate the particular culture originated in. Cateora states that some marketing studies have indicated that market niches are often better defined by similarities in geographic regions than by whole countries. For example, people who live in the "mega-cities" having populations of 10 million or more tend to have more in common with each other relating to product and service needs than with other people in their own country in small communities. Understanding the geographic background of a target market will help predict the response to a specific marketing mix.

The second role of geography in marketing decisions can directly affect product, packaging, and distribution plans. For example, regions of high humidity may require certain product modifications for functionality. Areas with difficult terrain will dictate packaging specifications and will have to be considered in distribution channel selection. The geographic factors of a new market cannot be assumed to be the same as one's familiar territory and cannot be overlooked without risk to the success of the marketing plan.

More information to be gathered concerning a new country market pertains to the country's infrastructure. One usually determines the state of the economic infrastructure, either through planning research or implementation. The degree of development of the transportation, energy, and communications infrastructure becomes obvious as a marketing strategy is put in place. It is much more advantageous to investigate the level of infrastructure available prior to implementation to avoid delays and major setbacks.

In addition to the economic infrastructure, what Drs. Czinkota and Ronkainen refer to as the social infrastructure will also impact the potential success of a marketing strategy. The effect of the social infrastructure—housing, health, and education is often not as obvious, however. Nevertheless, it will define what parts of a marketing strategy can and cannot be easily transported across borders. It will affect the level of demand, type and quality of product accepted, functional features needed, effective promotion plans, and even the appropriate means of production.

The education infrastructure is a good example to illustrate country differences. It is important to look at education beyond just which groups have it and which do not. Consider also what is emphasized in the structure. For instance, science and math is valued in Asian countries but, for the past forty years, hand labor and production was valued and promoted in the Eastern bloc countries. Health sciences and business mathematics were relegated to the lower echelon, and became low paying jobs. Knowledge of this infrastructure helps a marketer determine the value the people place on certain products; how they might be used and by whom; and what approach will appeal to the target market.

The structure of the social organization of the country can also be key information needed by the international marketer. The family structure and the types of relationships valued in the culture can be an important factor in product, promotion, and distribution decisions. A highly mobile, small family oriented market such as the United States will look for different product attributes than a mostly stationary, extended family oriented market such as in Mexico. Consider the trend setting areas in the United States, New York City and California. The many single people living alone and two income couples with no children have caused the initiation of such products as single serving pizza and individual frozen dinners. In a country where the social orientation is centered around large extended families sharing the main meal such products would find a tough market.

A slightly more subtle impact of the social organization is the determination of who is the real customer. In a structure such as that in Mexico, the relationship between a family and its patron, who may or may not be a relative, is highly valued. For many decisions, the patron is a strong influence, if not the decision maker, and thus needs to be considered as, at least, an intermediary in the distribution chain. Gaining an understanding of the inner workings of the social structure may help a marketer considerably shorten the customer's buying decision process, and can create relationships that become a competitive advantage.

Another infrastructure element that should be understood is what Czinkota and Ronkainen refer to as the financial infrastructure in the country. One needs to find out what can be financed, by whom, with what types of financing terms. Is financing government controlled, highly bureaucratic, only through banking institutions, entrepreneurial, or private? In countries such as Russia where financing is extremely complex and difficult, assisting a distributor in offering financial packages for a product may be a very valuable competitive edge.

The international marketer also needs to explore the country and regional laws specific to the marketplace. The international trade laws such as customs, tariffs, licensing, standards, local content, etc. should, of course, be well understood. However, the local laws can easily alter a marketing plan. Dr. Cateora indicates that there may be laws covering pricing, allowed mark-ups or discounts, exclusive territory agreements, distributor or wholesaler agreement establishment or cancellation, regulatory laws based on the country's history or objectives, intellectual property rights, etc. Consider how and where the local laws are typically enforced, and preferably, determine jurisdiction of contracts before signing agreements. Cateora and practicing attorneys suggest that an arbitration clause in a contract will identify the preferred arbitration agency before a dispute ever arises, thus simplifying any future issues.

Information that would seem the easiest to gather is the information concerning the country's political environment. The general stability of the government, the popularity of the incumbents, and the general direction of the country are usually covered by the world press. Other information important to a marketing plan, however, must be sought out. For example, what is the government's position toward business in general. and foreign business in particular. Are business leaders expected to be politically active? Are they expected to be involved in their community? Is the country's economic policy based on a government/industrial policy? What industries are subsidized? In what way? Consulates and embassies as well as industry associations and Chambers of Commerce can be sources of invaluable information pertaining to how government and business interwork within a country.

ORGANIZATION DESIGN

Once the country, culture, market, and environment are well understood, the international marketer can determine the optimal organizational structure to support the new market. The marketing structure must, of course, fit the overall organization as well as the new target market. Hence, the marketer must have a clear understanding of the corporation's goals and strategy and what role the new market is expected to play. Further, it is important to recognize how far along in the evolution of international marketing the corporation is. These factors significantly influence how the marketing organization should be structured to gain the best results.

It is generally observed that companies tend to evolve their organization and their marketing concept as their involvement in international business grows. To use the terminology of Dr. Philip Cateora, many companies begin by extending their domestic marketing, sales plans, and products to foreign customers. This is often prompted either by a customer who has opened an office in another country, or a desire to generate more volume for an existing product by expanding the number of potential customers. Dr. Cateora has classified this as the "ethnocentric" concept.

As the international business grows, the marketing concept tends to move to "polycentric" or multi-domestic. In this phase, the company sees the markets as unique local situations, and usually establishes independent foreign subsidiaries to meet the local requirements. This concept will typically grow the gross sales volumes for the corporation; but will also grow the costs associated with the sales through process duplication and customization. Ultimately, the company assumes a more global view and either accommodates certain cultural adaptation for specific markets—"regiocentric" concept, or looks for similar markets with the same requirements and characteristics around the world—"geocentric" concept.[1]

The organizational design supporting these marketing concepts evolves correspondingly. Drs. Czinkota and Ronkainen define the organizational evolution as moving from Multinational to Global. The multinational supports the polycentric concept through foreign subsidiaries operating autonomously. Next, usually as an efficiency move, the company will become "international" as the subsidiaries operate autonomously, but depend on the headquarters for processes and product. At this point, decisions pertaining to pricing, promotion, distribution, etc. are made locally in each country. The company usually then evolves to a global organization in which world-wide activities are closely managed through the central headquarters. Of course, there are many variations on these organization designs depending on the extent of local, regional, or global control over the various processes such as manufacturing, design, and staff functions such as personnel, besides the marketing functions.[2]

There is a new structure, identified by Bartlett and Ghoshal, that some companies are now evolving to with the support of the advancements in information technologies. Companies can now operate as transnational organizations. Using the world encompassing networks, high speed transmissions, and multimedia technologies, companies can optimize the synergy of the expertise and experience among the diverse personalities, backgrounds, and education of their people located anywhere. Teams can be created with members from experts groups from wherever they are needed. For example, a graphics artist in New York city can easily work with a sound artist in Nashville to support a copy writer and production manager in Mexico City to quickly develop a promotion for a Mexican distributor. Similarly, packaging engineering expertise may reside in an acquisition in Norway and support product designers in Germany or California. The management in a transnational organization have the ability and the infrastructure support to take a broad global view of the whole entity and capitalize on all of the corporation's assets, placing them in the most optimal locations. As Ives and Jarvenpaa define it, in the transnational organization, "global activities are integrated through close interdependence and cooperation among headquarters and foreign subsidiaries."[3]

A marketing organization structured transnationally provides the company flexibility and more effective decisions. By sharing information and expertise from all locations, the marketer gains faster information on changing trends, economic shifts, political change, etc. Leading edge products can be conceptualized, designed, and changed anywhere in the organization and sold throughout the world. With a global view, market segments can be defined as any group that has the same need and thus, the same response to the product, across the world. With this concept, market segments can be developed that are large enough to allow mass production with relatively little customization. Risk will be reduced with the improved information and increased ability to shift emphasis, attention, and product to the economically viable growth markets as they emerge throughout the world. Developing countries, with their small middle class and economic fluctuations, may not be viable markets for many companies. However, with a transnational strategy, companies can include emerging markets as one part of a world-wide segment and establish their presence in that market while spreading the risk over a significantly larger base. The company will be able to enter the market more quickly utilizing the interdependence of its elements in other countries, or may be able to build an element in the emerging country based on the knowledge that if it had to quickly pull out, the products and services developed there could be moved into other sites and continued. This sort of strategy requires continuous sharing of information, technologies, status, and planning. Bartlett and Ghoshal point out that broad cultural understanding and patience are also critical success factors in a transnational organization as people learn to depend on others with entirely different cultures and beliefs.

ECONOMIC INDICATORS

Once the country is studied and the organization determined, the international marketer can move to defining the marketing mix. One factor that plays a more fundamental role in an international strategy than a domestic one is the economics of the target country. The marketer can asses the general trends in the country and specific industry sectors via economic indicators. Without becoming an economics expert or forecaster, one can watch trends in certain indicators and gain a basic feeling for the general direction of the country market. For example, growth trends in GDP (gross domestic product) per capita is generally a good sign of growing buying power per person.

According to the Economist Guide, noting trends in imports / exports of a country can warn marketers of upcoming change. Sudden shifts increasing or decreasing a country's imports or exports can point to changes in inflationary trends. A significant increase in imports may indicate pent up demand that will drive up prices; or a sudden shift in exports may indicate government intervention to shore up the economy or foreign exchange pressures coming. Mexico's recent moves illustrate the point. An overvalued peso held constant by the country's reserves encouraged imports and held down inflation by holding down domestic wages and prices. The now devalued peso will spur exports and internal production with the "lower" prices on the world market but may trigger inflation as workers demand higher wages to equate the difference in buying power of the peso. Companies exporting to Mexico will now find a more difficult market. Companies already established in Mexico took a hit on their asset value, but may be better positioned to succeed in the longer run.

Major foreign exchange rate changes necessarily impact the marketing strategy. Does the corporation want to pass on higher "prices" to the distributors and get the distributors to swallow the cost, or pass it on to the customer—or does the company want to hold its competitive position and take the margin loss itself? These need to be conscious marketing decisions rather than left to be accounting functions.

MARKETING MIX

The international marketing mix itself must be closely integrated and supportive of the corporate vision and strategy. For example, a corporate objective of the long term development of a new country market will equate to a very different marketing plan than a short term strategy of moving excess inventory into a new market. Each element of the marketing mix affects the other, and all must be developed to support the overall corporate vision.

There are several general strategies that have been well discussed in marketing in past years: Market penetration to gain market share with existing products in existing markets; market development by moving existing products into new markets—often international markets; product development by creating a new product for a well known existing market; and diversification by creating a new product for a now market. The specific corporate strategy coupled with the previously mentioned corporate marketing concept of multi-domestic, international, global, or transnational all have major impact on the decisions regarding the marketing mix. The marketer must understand the strategic expectations that the specific marketing mix is to meet.

As Kuczmarski and Hulbert emphasize, it is helpful to establish a screening process to match opportunities to the strategy. The "screens" may include the fit with the corporate goals, existing competition in the market, market growth rate as well as the appropriateness to the values, culture, level of development, and needs in the country.

Product screening is equally important, and in some ways more difficult than general market screening. The parochial, cultural perception of the product designers and marketers may not reflect the true acceptability of the product in the new country. Cateora says that from the point of view of the new market culture, one must consider the relative advantage of the new product over the existing products or methods; the compatibility with accepted behavior, norms, values, and traditions; the complexity associated with the product's use; the economic or social risk associated with early adoption of the new product; and the ease with which the benefits of the new product can be explained and experienced. If it is economically and competitively feasible, market testing is one way of gaining a view of the product in the new culture. However, in many cultures, product testing is not easily done. Also, the validity of the test must be considered in light of the fascination with "newness" or the rejection of "foreign imports" or how different the product is to the normal modes of behavior. Thus, even with sensitively thought out product design and market testing, solid checks and measurements need to be established to monitor the true success or failure of the product to give enough time to make adjustments and changes.

Whenever possible, products should be designed as modular. This enables the benefits of "mass customization", as described by Joe Pine, in that core elements can be mass produced while certain elements can be customized per country or even per customer. Additionally, packaging, serviceability, and usability must be considered from the cultural point of view at the outset of product design.

The pricing element of the marketing mix is often overlooked as a strategic element even in domestic marketing. It can be a critical element in an international strategy. The international marketer needs to know the basics of international finance, currencies, economics, and inflationary impact to identify trends in markets, opportunities that competitors may miss, and potential for risk sharing. Consider, for example, the potential for cross border "gray markets". Cateora warns that if the price differential is wide enough in real or exchange amounts, third parties will buy product in one country and sell it in another— unauthorized. Until this is discovered, the company loses control of the product and service quality as well as the market penetration rate. It may also find itself in violation of existing distribution agreements if exclusive territories were defined. Thus, in general, the world market sets a price range for product types; consequently, the other elements of pricing and the marketing mix must be the competitive differentiators.

The total pricing structure of a product for a new country market depends on what the value is in the new country. Is the perceived value the same as in the domestic market or can certain things justify a premium? Hulbert suggests that the marketer consider service, volume discounts, return and repair management, buybacks, inventory management, freight, delivery preparation, etc. all as part of the pricing strategy. Further, the marketer must establish the pricing policies. How much price flexibility should be delegated to the local distributors— carte blanche pricing, within a given range, or an inflexible set price?

Again, one must think of the cultural differences regarding bargaining, barter, and discounting. Few countries in the world respect a set price as in the United States.

Other aspects of pricing are built into the cost of the product. Can costs be modular so that unnecessary overhead is not built into a transfer price and then added on again in the new country via payments to shippers, advertisers, distributors, etc.? How does the distribution chain price its services? Consider product assembly costs. Can some parts be purchased cheaper in the new country and added at the point of final distribution? Integrating all elements of the marketing mix— product, price, promotion, and distribution—is critical to being competitive.

Financing is an additional element of the pricing/promotion/ distribution mix that is often an essential part of moving product into a new country market. Providing financing for distributors and customers may be critical to establishing a presence in a new market. Cateora identifies the normal means of financing as including letters of credit, a bill of exchange between the buyer's and seller's banks, partial cash in advance, or open accounts for long standing customers. Special arrangements may be counter trade including providing equipment and receiving payment in goods or services supplied with equipment sold, or third party payment in other goods or currencies. For example, in the telecommunications industry it is feasible to provide telephone switching equipment and receive payment as telephone service in the new country. Czinkota and Ronkainen describe other arrangements which may include a debt for debt swap between creditors in which a bank will assume the seller's debt in exchange for the buyer's debt and vice versa. A debt for equity arrangement occurs when the seller provides product or service in exchange for equity in the distributor or customer's business. Other debt swaps even include things such as personnel training on site for product, or offering test sites for product, etc.

Financing can be a creative means of establishing a competitive differentiation. As discussed by Cateora, Czinkota and Ronkainen, several agencies and institutions assist companies in backing various financing arrangements. Factoring houses buy receivables at discount. Many third parties, such as large international banks, buy promissory notes at a discount that are guaranteed by the importer's bank. Companies can use the Eximbank to guarantee loans from correspondent banks for financing; and use OPIC, Overseas Private

Investment Corporation, to finance direct investment in developing countries.

The element of the marketing mix most affected, next to the product or service itself, by culture and values is promotion. One of the first points to consider in the promotional decisions for a new country market is the degree of "newness" perceived by the intended market. Is the product or service a new brand of something familiar, a new way of doing something well known, or is it something never before seen in the market? Does the promotion have to familiarize or educate people to something in order to introduce the product or service? Will it fit with the normal cultural behavior? The marketer must consider whether the company has the commitment and desire to be a cultural "change agent" if the product will cause entirely different action than normal behavior would dictate. Examples of such situations include infant formula sold in Africa where potable water was not readily accessible or contraceptives sold in Mexico where the religious and family culture forbids birth control. Cultural ethics and judgment are essential competencies needed by the international marketer not only in determining if the product fits the market at all, but also how to introduce and promote it.

Language, of course, is a key factor in developing promotional material. Additionally, however, the marketer needs to consider what Urban and Hauser refer to as the customer's psychological profile for the appropriate promotional message. From that customer's point of view, what are the key differentiators and benefits of the product or service? What is important and valued in that culture?

Besides the perception of the product, the customer has certain cultural expectations and perceptions of the promotional process itself. For example, what is the perception of imported products in general— from that specific domestic country? Is it better to capitalize on a world brand name, such as Coca Cola; or would the product be perceived more positively for the specific market with a unique name to enhance the newness and adaptation? How does the customer expect to be "sold"? Telemarketing, for example, is a fairly well accepted promotional technique in the United States but would be ineffective or even resented in many other country markets. Some markets expect to deal only with the producer while others depend on the local distributor to advise and counsel customers in the purchasing decision. Further, the customer's expectations may be different depending on the type of product or industry being considered.

Another facet of promotion the marketer must be familiar with is the local law regarding promotion. Laws may restrict a company's expenditures on advertising, limit the media allowed for certain products, require that company ownership or original manufacturer be identified clearly, or insist that only products that are immediately available can be advertised. In some countries advertisement will have to pass censors before being allowed. It is best to know such requirements long before the publication deadline nears.

Ultimately, the international marketer must determine the optimum distribution for the product in the target country market. As in any market, the first step is to find out how the customer buys such products, from whom, and where. What services should a distributor be able to provide? Services that may be required can include customer training, financing, inventory stocking, and even currency exchange for the end customer.

Local law as well as international law must again be known when developing distributor agreements. Additionally, however, the international marketer may need to consider such things as how technologically adept the potential distributor is. Do the producer's current systems meet the distributor's needs or do they overwhelm the distributor. Does the distributor require more sophisticated systems support?

In the new country market culture, what are the best incentives for distributors and sales people? Some cultures such as the United States are best incented monetarily through price discounts, bonuses, cash awards, etc. Other cultures, such as the Mexican culture, may be incented more by paid reward travel or bonus vacation time. Still other cultures may resent incentive rewards of any type and instead expect advancement, equity, etc. for meeting or exceeding expectations of the producer. The knowledgeable international marketer recognizes that one cannot create a sales plan that will fit all cultures and markets.

Various agencies and organizations can assist a company in finding distributors, freight forwarders, etc. specializing in the target country. The United States Department of Commerce, the country's Chambers of Commerce, other manufacturers, and even freight carriers are good sources to use when searching for distributors and agents.

Most authors mention and Urban and Hauser particularly emphasize that once the marketing mix is formulated, the entire integrated plan should be tested. An alternative to extensive and costly market tests in the new country where the company is not yet established can be consultants, university groups, and focus groups. Most large U.S. universities have a substantial international representation in the student body, and many have international centers and organizations willing to assist in market tests. In conducting the market tests, it is essential to also build in the measurements to determine success. The measurements should monitor the elements in support of the overriding goals and objectives of the corporation discussed at the beginning. A goal of long-term market development of an entirely new country market cannot be measured by short-term return on sales. Percentage growth in year over year sales and market share may be much more appropriate measurements for the objective. The key point is to gain agreement in the company as to the objectives and the measurements, test the measurements in the trials to ensure that they are obtainable and meaningful, and then track the results, and adjust the strategies as required.

No matter how much "up-front" work is done, a new country market with a new culture will create surprises. Build in the flexibility and remain sensitive to the need to adjust.

NOTES

1. Cateora, P.R.; *International Marketing,* 7th edition; Irwin Press; p. 21-25.

2. Czinkota, M.F., and Ronkainen, I.A., *International Marketing,* 2nd edition; Dryden Press; p. 639-652.

3. Ives, B. & Jarvenpaa, S.; "Wiring the Stateless Corporation: Empowering the Drivers and Overcoming the Barriers"; INSIGHT for SIM.

CHAPTER II

The Big "C" Within the 4 P's (Product, Price, Promotion, & Place)

TECHNOLOGY

A tremendous force impacting marketing strategies and techniques, as well as all aspects of business management and process, is the exponential advancement and penetration of information communications technologies. "Communication", (the BIG C,) of massive amounts of information is possible through the rapid proliferation of increasingly powerful technologies—in computing capabilities, storage devices, data compression equipment, transmission devices and media as well as management software to direct and control information transfers.

In the United States, the technological advancements permeate every aspect of daily living. Without going into detail about specific areas of technology, listing a few major categories will illustrate the tremendous growth. For example, the continuous evolution of processor speeds and computing capacity through such things as parallel processing has enabled the concept of client/ server networks. This combination of powerful individual computing capability in the client workstation coupled with the centralized storage and communications capabilities of the server-based information data bases enable individuals to access and, more important, utilize current, dynamic, key

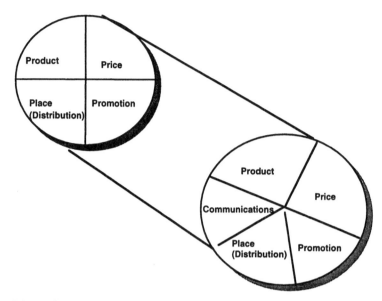

Figure 2. The four "P's" of Marketing Strategy plus Information 'Communications.

information in their daily work. Information such as financial balances, inventory listings, or customer transactions that were available only monthly or, at best, weekly can now be up to date instantly.

The broader application of this computing ability to information types other than data has now provided the individual user with "multimedia" capability. A person at a desk-top workstation is able to create applications that incorporate sound, images, graphics, voice, and even video to more effectively utilize and present information. As recently as five years ago, such applications required massive computers and programmers with years of specialized experience.

Adding to these advances the rapid enhancements of communications technologies has given people the ability to transfer these complex applications and important information to other people nearly anywhere in the world today. Communication of sophisticated programs and information, which five to ten years ago, was only possible over expensive, private, corporate networks is now occurring daily around the world through a loosely tied together system of networks known as the Internet. The World Wide Web system of pointers can help an individual find a data base of information on one of hundreds of servers located throughout the world in a relatively short period of time. Started by university scientists collaborating on research, the Internet has now gained the attention of major corporations as a means of communicating not only among geographically dispersed corporate offices, but also to external corporate partners as well as to a wide spread customer base.

The ongoing development of communications technologies will continue to enhance the usability of networks and consequently, of information. Consider the advances of fiber optic cable as a communications media. The capacity of a single strand of fiber has tripled every ten years so that today thousands of individual telephone calls can be simultaneously transmitted over one fiber. The distance of fiber transmission before a repeat of the signal is required has advanced from once being only three miles to now allowing transmission across the Atlantic Ocean. This means the cost of inserting expensive electronic repeating equipment under the ocean can be eliminated. The enhancements in the capacity, speed, and distance of transmission over fiber means that in the near future, a multimedia video signal will be sent to the other side of the world in milliseconds and a traditional voice telephone call to another hemisphere will hardly be noticed on the networks.

Then, one must also consider the rapid advances being made in wireless transmission technologies. Antennae are becoming sophisticated enough to screen out noise and receive voice signals clearly on relatively low-speed spectrum, thus reducing costs. As the quality of the transmitting signals increases, the speed of the switching equipment increases, and the receiving abilities of the antennae increase, wireless interactive multimedia applications will become possible. The result will be the ability to open even the nearly unreachable spots of the world to sophisticated communications. In 1994, for example, Argentina was able to install and activate a nation-wide cellular telephone network—a $5 Billion investment—in 120 days. The constraints of having to physically place wire across mountains and plains to reach each home and business were removed.

Besides the processing and transmission capability enhancements, there have been tremendous advances made in the software that directs the processing. Modular system programs such as hypertext allow the applications creator to build amazing flexibility into highly sophisticated applications. As Marsh and Vanston explain, in hypertext systems, the ultimate end user of the applications can then utilize the system in the sequence that is the most meaningful. Pointers interconnect modules and data in innumerable ways so the sequence of use does not have to be linear. Used in educational applications, hypertext ability allows a student to progress through an interactive course, for example, in a manner that best meets the individual interest. One can imagine that a course might be studied in a very different sequence if the student were interested in archeology or zoology. Similarly, hypertext modularity is critical when the application is a scenario modeling tool or a business process system model. A model would be used in a very different sequence if the "student" were a purchasing manager rather than a manufacturing specialist. In the not too distant future, modular systems will "learn" as they progress through different paths—building new potential connections and new solutions each time they are used. It is easy to begin to speculate on the power of such a modeling tool.

ROLE OF TECHNOLOGY IN MARKETING

The advances in and convergence of computing and communications technologies are so powerful and rapid that they seem to be out of anyone's control. How can a marketer begin to harness the technological capabilities available and use them to optimize a marketing strategy? As Haeckel and Nolan point out, the first step is the same as when developing the strategy. The marketer must understand the business and how it functions and have a clear picture of the corporate vision and objectives as discussed in the first chapter. Be careful not to "automate" just to automate.

The use of information technology in marketing will be quite different depending on whether the corporation considers itself multinational, global, or transnational. Is the corporate objective to build long term relationships with customers, with distributors, with suppliers, in foreign markets, or is the goal to expand the market to use excess plant capacity? Does the company have a specific target of how much revenue should be gained from new products or is the goal to capitalize on the profitability of existing standard products? These differing objectives will guide the marketer into the types of systems that can assist various activities—from sharing global customer files across a transnational organization to building automated ordering systems for distributors.

Once the marketer has gained a clear understanding of the corporate vision, it is important to analyze the systemic interrelationship of functions and how each interacts with and supports the next to reach the corporate vision. Most corporations in the industrialized world have fairly extensive information systems. Typically technology has been introduced in the financial and control areas, manufacturing plants, inventory systems, and perhaps customer information files in sales. In the majority of companies, however, these systems are not considered marketing information systems, as indicated by Haeckel and Nolan. Nevertheless, they are exactly that. When the systemic interrelationship is considered, the customer data bases, inventory management systems, manufacturing process definitions, and financial systems all pull together around the ultimate customer sale. In most cases, the many systems already built are not compatible or interconnected since they usually originated independently. However, for most companies, the information exists and what is required is a base infrastructure to take advantage of it—as will be discussed.

When the interrelationships are defined, and the corporate objectives clear, the marketer must still determine the desired behavior outcome of a specific implementation of technology in marketing. An easy example of behavior impacting implementation is the technology supporting telemarketing centers. If the desired behavior is that the telemarketing staff call or answer as many customers as possible in a day, the technology will be set up to route calls to any available agent, automatically call potential customers when an agent station is idle, time the length of calls, etc. On the other hand, if the desired behavior is to provide personal customized service to calling customers, the same technology will be set up to route calls to product specialist agents based on the number called, link the call to customer files to ensure the agent has the customer background, and perhaps interconnect the system to the inventory system to highlight products that could be on special sale. Knowing the desired behavior outcome is critical to the initial design of technology implementation.

Equally important is building in the measurements to ensure that the objectives are being met and the flexibility that allows the systems to be adjusted and changed as the environment or objectives change. Well thought out, modular systems enable the marketer to adjust information sources, alter implementation objectives, react to new competitive strategies, and meet new customer demands. Haeckel and Nolan indicate that a marketing system built inflexibly to work from static information in today's changing dynamic business environment is more damaging to the corporation's long term health than no marketing system.

USE OF INFORMATION COMMUNICATIONS IN MARKETING

There are numerous examples of the use of information communications in marketing written up in articles in both marketing journals as well as technology journals. The fact that many of the examples are still considered anomalies is probably due to the significant challenges faced when implementing a marketing system. Before considering the challenges, first think of the many potential uses.

As in financial and operational systems, marketing systems first began in an introverted manner—for internal use in the corporations. Today, the most obvious use of information communications systems in marketing is still market research. Customer data bases can be built from information collected periodically in such ways as customer surveys, distributor questionnaires, purchased industry studies, and even customized, purchased consultant studies. As Joe Pine discusses, more and more, customer information is now collected in an on-going manner from customer transactions. Linkages with order-entry and inventory and shipping systems as well as accounts receivable systems will update on-line customer files with the customer's most current data. For instance, a customer's product or service preferences or change in preferences can be quickly identified and provided to sales along with the customer's normal buying frequency, updated address and telephone, credit history, and any service requests or complaints. One global hotel chain, for example, keeps preferred customers in a centralized data base and even instantly updates a customer's room service order. When the customer next registers at a hotel in the chain anywhere in the world, the hotel staff pleasantly surprises the guest by verifying personalized requests even before being asked.

Data bases such as this can be analyzed in a variety of ways to provide valuable market data. An analysis of customers' purchases over time can enable a marketer to more closely predict the seasonality of products or other interdependencies on external factors such as the lead or lag time to economic swings. An analysis of purchases by geography over time may give the marketer early warning to the entry of competition if steady customers begin to delay normal re-purchases. Depending on the amount and depth of customer information collected, a correlation analysis of important data may help the marketer more finely segment markets based on better understanding of customer characteristics matched to customer requirements. For example, doctors in clinics with more than three physicians in cities of 100,000 or less population may request a specific packaging size and type of a given supply product.

Internal data bases on competitors and competitive activity are more difficult to create, but can provide equally valuable market information. As with customer information, competitive data can be gained from secondary research sources such as industry association studies, consultant reports, or customized consulting studies. Companies often overlook excellent internal sources of competitive information, however. Providing direct sales personnel or distributors with access to the system and an incentive to complete questionnaires or post competitive information will usually facilitate the data base creation. Once obtained, this data base can also be analyzed in a variety of ways. Competitive activity compared geographically may indicate the competitor's strategy for market expansion. Again depending on the amount and depth of the information, other analyses can provide different insight; for example, a sudden surge in sales of a particular model of product by the competitor may indicate a major sale of that model pending a new model introduction. Of course, the marketer must be cautious not to read too much into analyses and be certain the data is accurate and current.

The current growth of on-line data bases are offering new sources for market research at relatively low cost. Several companies such as Compuserv, America On-Line, and Dow Jones Retrieval provide customers with access to specialized data bases of business and news information, kept up to date on a daily basis. Additionally, these on-line services also offer gateways to the Internet which then opens up access to servers holding information all around the world—particularly in universities. Some of the companies offer a clipping service for customers, allowing the customer to select topics for which the service will scan newspapers and periodicals on a daily or weekly basis. The customized data base of requested information is then placed in the customers "mail box" for convenient access. The U.S. government now maintains several servers of public access information including such things as census data and congressional bills available on the Internet. Most of the on-line services are primarily collecting U.S. publication information; however, Compuserv and Dow Jones Retrieval are beginning to collect some international periodicals.

Another form of research becoming available via the communications technologies is electronic "brainstorming." Marketers in far flung corporate locations can gather regional market information and then collaborate in a world-wide brainstorming session. If the locations are in the same hemisphere and time zones are not an issue, these research/strategy sessions can be conducted via multi-site video conference arrangements. If the groups transverse multiple time zones making same-time video meetings impossible, the groups can utilize special conferencing software on a server. The conferencing system allows participants to enter ideas and comments in an organized manner in text at any time. The text/graphics messages are stored chronologically within topic so that the other people can read everyone's comments and ideas, add their own and continue the conversation. Since the messages continue to be stored in the system and can be saved on each individual's computer and/or printed, the ideas and information are not lost and can be referred to again and again. Such conferencing systems can, of course, be used for many purposes beyond market research and strategy including such things as focus groups to test new promotional campaigns or even products and services in various locations.

A second use of information communications that began with individuals within a company and has expanded to networked systems is desktop publishing. As workstations grew more powerful and gained multimedia capability, marketing communications specialists began developing promotional material internally. In most cases the internal development could be faster, easier to incorporate changes and product updates, and less costly. With network enhancements, today's corporate marketing communications personnel can now receive full color advertising graphics from ad agencies for review and approval, send camera-ready layouts to printers, and develop complete promotional campaign material which is then networked to a distributor's printer for on the spot flyers and literature. As an example, one large soft drink producer monitors sales from distributors to manage inventory of a short shelf-life product. If the weather was poor over a holiday weekend in one part of the country and the distributors are left with too much stock on hand, the producer will create special promotional ads, flyers, and coupons and network the camera-ready material to newspapers in the area on Monday. By the evening edition of the Monday paper, the distributors in the affected area can be offering sales on the soft drink to move inventory before obsolescence. The benefits of the system are enormous—reduced time and cost of promotional creative work, increased sales, reduced returned product, and perhaps most important, happier and thus loyal distributors.

As internal corporate networks expand in reach and capacity, marketing systems have also expanded. Product announcements and news releases can be broadcasted to all employees around the world, keeping everyone up to date on the company's accomplishments. Such networks become news sources and can be used to inform employees of major sales won, corporate acquisitions, competitive information, etc. Unfortunately, too few companies have discovered the advantages of sharing marketing, sales, and competitive information with all of the employees. Fred Smith of Federal Express is one CEO who has discovered the key advantages. He has stated in a speech at the American Quality Association conference that gaining satisfied customers follows having satisfied and happy employees, and having satisfied, happy employees comes from communications—helping people feel connected and truly part of the whole company. This type of communications is critical in a truly transnational corporation.

Federal Express also uses their corporate world-wide network for training employees. Although this is seldom considered a marketing function, it is certainly one of the key functional interdependencies the marketer needs to recognize. Product and service training for sales and support personnel is a critical element of any distribution plan. With advanced information communications systems, highly sophisticated and complex products and services can be explained and demonstrated to employees anywhere in the world. All of the employees can have access to the most up to date information regarding the newest product at the same time. As the network expands, such training can be offered as one of the negotiating points in distributor contracts as well.

When the sophistication of hypertext is added to marketing systems, the potential for creating market scenarios becomes available. Scenario planning has been recognized as a powerful strategic tool for a long time; however, systems are now becoming available to allow most companies the ability to use the tool. In scenario planning, the corporation's various experts from technology, product design, marketing, finance, etc. can enter all sorts of possible future events likely to occur in their area of expertise into the system. In a hypertext mode, various combinations and permutations can be put together. The company can then think through their optimal course of action given the potential future scenarios. According to Peter Senge of MIT, Royal Dutch Shell used such a planning technique to prepare their response in case of an oil crisis. Consequently, they were the best prepared and situated when the OPEC crisis actually occurred. Is it a marketing function? Strategic planning must be based on what the market is expected to do. Which functional group in the company drives the system becomes irrelevant—everyone must contribute to the scenarios to make them viable.

As corporations begin to make their system extroverted, significant advantages become possible with marketing systems. Extroverted systems link the company with outside groups such as customers, distributors, vendors, and partners. When these linkages are coupled with the many internal information systems, whole new concepts arise. Consider the new movement towards "mass customization" as defined by Joe Pine—gaining the benefits of mass production while providing the customer with customized products. Such a concept is only possible when many sources of information are systematically available. Customer requests coming to distributors must be directly linked to production planning systems which need to be linked to purchasing systems, supplier systems, inventory systems, shipping systems, etc. At the same time, the information needs to be available for market analysis to determine trends in customer requests to build the appropriate product design modules to enable the "customization" on a mass produced basis.

Although the total mass customization concept is new and few companies have implemented the entire capability, several companies have been moving in the direction. At the Institute for Information Studies sessions Benneton was often given as an example of a company using information communications to gain significant competitive advantages. Benneton's store systems feed sales information to the production sites on an on-going basis. The system can indicate, for example, that lilac sweaters and scarves are suddenly a big seller in New York. The production will quickly shift to producing lilac dye lots and getting product shipped to New York. Since this can happen, literally, overnight, the entire Benneton process must be interlinked to facilitate such actions. Many of Benneton's products are produced in natural yarns so they can be colored as needed by the market. The product line is "designed" with modularity to build in the flexibility; and the communications and data collection systems feed in the information to indicate the appropriate product mix for the volatile market. Haeckel and Nolan point out that it is critical in such systems, that the initial system design be based on basic knowledge of the market, the industry, and the company's operations. The criteria built into the systematized decisions are essential. They must consider market trends, seasonality, operational functions, etc. In other words, the systems only work if they are designed by the people who fully understand the business.

To build toward such an all encompassing system, many companies begin in smaller steps. For example, networked marketing systems can provide all sales channels with immediately up-dated pricing, inventory status of all warehouses and estimated shipping times from the various locations, suggested substitutions for any out of stock or discontinued items, other distributors with available stock, parts suppliers in the local area, etc.—all information that enables the sales personnel to meet the customer request in the fastest possible time.

Additionally, as Bessen indicates, interlinked systems continuously updating marketing systems with customer preferences and characteristics, supplier information, sales statistics, etc. can be used to create and improve criteria in the company's decision systems. Usually it is assumed that systems that track customer purchasing preferences are retail systems that capture data at the cash register. However, equally valuable information can be captured through the sales channel about any customer transaction. If the company sells complex specialized equipment to other industrial companies, for example, customer information can be garnered from the order entry system, the customer service representatives, training personnel, as well as the direct sales personnel. Each time contact is made with the customer it can be technologically "remembered". An analysis of customer history files can then indicate many things such as what products are high turnovers, what is the failure rate of certain OEM parts based on service calls, what is the best product shipment methods, which are the top 20% customers and what annual volume do they buy of which products, etc. Such systems are invaluable to corporations whether they are retailing mass merchandise or selling highly sophisticated, specialized products and services to the business community.

In international marketing, systems that can support the sales channels with specific customer information, giving the customer's background, preferences, buying history, etc. can help the sales person build the relationship so crucial in many cultures such as in Latin America. "Micro-marketing" systems that simplify product choices by matching the customer needs and preferences to specific product offerings in personalized letters, for example, can facilitate the job of the sales person in attending the specific customer's need. However, caution is needed to avoid over-systematizing the personal interface between the company and the customer. As is often said but too often forgotten—"People buy from people."

With the technological and geographical growth of the Internet, many corporate marketers are looking to the Internet as an electronic distribution channel besides a research tool as mentioned previously. This new form of distribution must be considered cautiously, however, as several companies have discovered. Internet users form a culture of their own, and have become absolutely incensed over some corporations' attempts to commercialize the "net" by blatantly advertising or selling over it. A more subtle approach does seem to be accepted and even appreciated, however. As an example, a large personal computer hardware and software manufacturer has placed a server containing a catalog of all of its products on the "net". Although actual sales are still made through the existing channels, the company has discovered that many of its customers are accessing the server catalog prior to talking with the sales people to be knowledgeable about the trends, directions, and newest offerings. No attempt has yet been made to attribute any sales directly to this new form of subtle "advertising"; but since the company is taking more formal steps to ensure the server information is being maintained, one can expect that its usefulness will be measured. As the Internet becomes increasingly ubiquitous around the world and easier for the casual user to access, more multinational companies will begin to capitalize on the potential for product and service exposure to a self-defined market—those who actually proactively seek the information.

There are, of course, some companies that do support electronic purchasing. Although still a small segment of the purchasing population, "on-line" sales are expected to rapidly grow. In the business community certain commodity items are automatically ordered when the inventory stock reaches a specified minimum level. The computer information system can generate a standardized purchasing order and upon command—usually triggered by a person overseeing the system—the purchasing order will be transmitted over the network to a pre-established receiving vendor. The vendor's system is also programmed to accept the same standardized format for the purchasing orders and enters the order into the production system. If the transaction data is stored in a customer file, the vendor should have a significant advantage over other vendors to anticipate the customer's requirements, and to quickly generate a list of potential customers most likely to purchase new model supplies or new products introduced into the product line. The challenge, of course, is to maintain the personal contact with each customer as well since service is usually the differentiator among vendors offering commodity products on-line.

In the mass consumer market, some companies are venturing into the on-line ordering systems for their technologically advanced customers. After an unsuccessful start ten years ago, banks are once again beginning to offer at-home, on-line banking services such as account balance verification, payments, and funds transfers. Joe Pine gives an example of one company that has begun offering subscriber customers a system for on-line grocery shopping. Partnering with two large grocery chains, this company provides daily updated lists of items available in the stores, including sale specials, bonus buys, et.al. Subscribers order through the system, and the company has a staff that purchases the items and delivers them to the customer's home. With each order, the system asks how the company performed on the last order and logs suggestions or complaints to both improve service as well as update that customer's preferences. An easily foreseen next step for this company would be for it to partner with other retail outlets besides groceries and begin offering other products and services to its customers.

In similar ways, marketing information communications systems often evolve into an additional use—that of being a product themselves. For over a decade already, companies have sorted and dissected customer lists and sold the information to other companies in need of market segment information for market research or direct mail campaigns. As the data bases become more sophisticated and the segments become more finely defined, the information becomes more valuable. Corporations that "micro-market" niche products and services purchase well analyzed customer lists to limit costs of contact and gain the best return for the investment.

Besides customer information, other types of marketing information can also turn into valuable products and services. The large credit card companies that now offer their customers itemized summaries of purchases could re-sort the information and provide manufacturers with sales analyses per product by demographics, geography, season, or other break outs. The company described above that offers the grocery service could become a broker for other companies over the existing system and gain a transaction fee from both the purchasing customer as well as the retailer or manufacturer offering the products.

Sometimes information gathering devices can become excellent sales tools. One example is the computer chip being inserted into tires by a retreading company. The chip records tire revolutions and inflation levels. Besides being a performance quality measurement, the information also serves as an indicator to the customer when new tires are required. Would such a product quality measurement idea be considered a marketing information communications system? Probably not; and this is one of the major challenges to marketers in optimizing information communications technologies in marketing strategies.

CHALLENGES

A major challenge facing marketers in building technological marketing systems is the lack of infrastructure—physical and logical infrastructure both within the corporation and in the public networks. Infrastructure, in this case, is referring to all of the necessary underlying technologies and organizational policies that enable the collection and transmission of the information. As previously mentioned, for most corporations the luxury of creating a whole new system from scratch does not exist. Multiple systems already exist, usually specialized in function such as inventory management systems, customer billing systems, etc. Since these systems were typically created independently at different times, they are most often incompatible. Significant investment is required to retrofit or, often, redesign the systems into a cohesive whole for the uses discussed above. In most companies, the marketing function cannot make such an investment alone. A visionary leader is required at the top of the corporation who can see the potential value of such a system for the company's future, and who will make the financial and time commitment needed.

At the Institute for Information Studies roundtable, the discussion often centered around how a company justifies the investment in a corporate wide information network. The participating executives indicated in their conversations that the process often began with some small, highly visible and successful projects. The example of the desktop publishing/advertising creation system of the soft drink company was such a project. However, although individual projects could demonstrate the value of such systems, they could not justify a world-wide corporate network. The commitment to create that extensive infrastructure usually came as a "leap of faith" from an insightful, future-oriented president or CEO.

Beyond the need for the physical technology investment, the marketer also must create the view of the marketing system as an integrating tool that can positively impact product design and development, manufacturing, sales and operations as well as strategic planning. All of these functions have normally been thought of as discrete separate steps in the company's processes. A broader, holistic view is required to see the need for interactively sharing the information from one function with the others. For most hierarchical structured companies that began in the 50's and 60's, accepting this integrated systemic view is a cultural change. Integration across functions is again a commitment that marketing may help stimulate but that requires a leader at the top of the organization to make. Such a change in corporate values, culture, and ultimately organizational behavior must begin before a technology implementation. A system design must be based on the corporate values; it cannot create or change them. As more corporations move toward a transnational organizational structure to optimize their resources for the world-wide markets, the need for shared information communications systems will become more apparent, and the marketer's "selling" job a little easier.

Given that the internal corporate commitment is made, another significant challenge to the creation of an information communications network is the public network technology. Business people anywhere in the world today are fully aware of the advances in information and communications technologies. In some parts of the world, however, taking advantage of the power of the technologies is difficult if not impossible for an individual company because the public network infrastructure is not adequate. As people begin using advanced systems as described above, including multimedia and graphics, the requirements for communications quickly surpass the capacity of many public networks. Video conferencing quality is marginally acceptable even over some parts of the U.S. networks. If the maximum transmission speed provided to a given location for video conferencing is only two "56000 bits per second" lines, for instance, the video conferencing quality will most likely be disappointing. In many major cities in the world, it is impossible to obtain two such dedicated lines to any location. A company site with many employees using multimedia systems that need to communicate over a network will require tremendous amounts of transmission bandwidth at high speed. These requirements are still difficult to obtain and very expensive.

Progress is being made, however, in availability and quality of network capacity throughout the world. In most countries, the public network is being privatized and opened to competition. As demonstrated over the last two decades in the United States, competition among network providers ultimately results in significant growth in capacity and services and reduction in prices. In the U.S., for example, long distance voice calls can now be made for as little as $.10 per minute, and some businesses even get service as low as $.06-7 per minute, as compared to $.80 per minute or more not so long ago. Competition in other countries is expected to cause similar results. In Mexico, for example, all of the major U.S. long distance companies have already formed partnerships and/or have made commitments of large dollar investments to begin building long distance networks throughout the country. Simultaneously, the growth in cellular capacity and reach has been exponential. Thus, as Mott explains for Arthur Andersen's Sourcebook, although the government mandate to the previously government owned telephone company, TELMEX, was that they must increase penetration of telephone line availability to 8.6% from 5% of the population by 1994, it is expected that service availability exceeds the mandate and will continue to grow due to cellular capacity and land-line competition. Nevertheless, before the marketer makes a commitment to an international marketing information communications system, it would be wise to ensure the physical capability is available first.

Another challenge that must not be overlooked in the development of marketing information communications systems is ensuring security of the information sent through the system. Most software designed to create data bases provide fairly elaborate hierarchies of passwords. System designers can set up the data bases so that they can be altered or updated by designated people, accessed and read by other people, and completely inaccessible by still others. However, considering the sophistication of equipment now available that can randomly generate and test potential passwords for people trying to illegally access data, and equipment that can tap into network transmission and "read" data as it is transmitted, many information communications systems managers are now using specialized encoding schemes. Called encryption devices, equipment is now readily available that will encode data being sent over a network. Once encoded, that data can only be decoded by equipment using the same encryption scheme. Thus, even if data is captured as it is passed over a network, it is unreadable and thus useless to those who illegally gathered it. As marketing information systems become more integrated into the operations of the business and more valuable as marketing tools and sales aids, it behooves the marketer to take extra precaution to secure the information as a highly valuable asset of the company.

CHAPTER III

The 4 P's Within the Even Bigger "C"—Culture

A consideration that will have perhaps the most critical impact on the success or failure of an international marketing strategy is the sensitivity to and compatibility with the culture of the new foreign market. The culture of a people is firmly grounded in the values of that people; and a marketing strategy that intentionally or inadvertently thwarts those values will fail. At best, it will be simply noted for its inappropriateness and ignored. At worst, it will be sabotaged and destroyed.

VALUES

Values are the concepts that are highly esteemed in a society. They are beliefs that are kept sacred and passed from generation to generation. It would seem that these core beliefs upon which every aspect of the society is based would be fairly easily determined. Yet it seems that the majority of companies observe a society's customs; some take time to study the culture; but few ever truly try to understand the underlying values driving everything else. Perhaps, because one's own values are so deeply ingrained, it is difficult to imagine that other societies could be based on different values. However, it is these deep beliefs that create the culture that causes people to act as they do; and more important, to react as they do to "foreign" companies, new products and services, and marketing strategies.

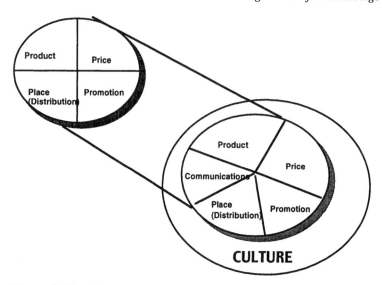

Figure 3. The elements of Marketing Strategy within a Culture.

In attempting to identify another people's values, it is important to fully understand one's own so as to be able to note the differences. A study conducted by James O'Toole at the University of Southern California has identified four primary values of Western democratic society—particularly the United States. The four values are Liberty, Equality, Efficiency, and Community or the Quality of Life. These are the things that people want in their life, and normally, they want as much of each as possible. However, even within a single society, individuals place different levels of importance on the different values which creates considerable misunderstandings and great conflicts. For instance, someone who believes that liberty is the most critical aspect of life will be at direct odds with a person who believes that some freedoms must be sacrificed in order to equalize opportunity for everyone. Similarly, a person who seeks the greatest efficiency in everything from products to processes will have great difficulty understanding the motives of a person who is willing to give up an aspect of efficiency to improve the aesthetics and attractiveness of something. People involved in developing a marketing strategy that includes product design, packaging, pricing, and promotion can have major disagreements around the importance of one value over another.

When it is essential for them to understand the perspective and values of another society to predict reaction to the marketing mix, we can see how difficult it is to identify and incorporate the values of the target market people.

Values are learned in early life experiences from the example and teachings of other people, mostly the immediate family. But where do they come from? According to O'Toole, the identified values of Western thought have been traced at least back to the great philosophers such as Aristotle and Socrates. For example, the importance of liberty and freedom most likely stems from the ancient practice of slavery. Conquering peoples forced those who were defeated into slavery and treated them as if they were animals of burden, or worse. In such circumstances, it was easy to learn the tremendous value of liberty and ingrain the importance of it in each generation of liberty. When one considers the beginnings of the Caucasian settlements and the government of the United States, the emphasis placed on liberty, freedom, and hence, individualism becomes apparent. The first settlers from England came to the newly found country because they valued liberty over any of the other aspects of life.

In Eastern societies where slavery was not practiced as it was in the West, liberty and individual freedom are not considered in the same way. Eastern tradition teaches that all elements of the Universe are interconnected. Mankind is part of the whole, and each person is connected with and therefore impacts each other person and the world around them as well. One can note that in the Eastern languages, the concept of separate individuals does not exist. It cannot even be described in their words.

The value of "Community" in the high "context" society such as Latin America surprisingly probably originates from the extremely defined caste system known to have been part of the advanced Aztec and Mayan civilizations and certainly enforced by the western European conquerors. This value of Community—of taking care of one's neighbor—corresponds well with the cultural aspect of Power Distance as defined by Geert Hofstede. Power Distance defines a hierarchical system in the society, in organizations, in most all aspects of the people's interactions. Although the system may be resented by those not at the power levels, it is expected that those "in power" have the responsibility of taking care of the others. One can recall the Medieval feudal system for a clear picture of the Lord in the castle protecting the peasant community in the valley which in turn supplied the Lord and his court with life's necessities. As the value evolved over centuries, it is still visible today. In countries such as Mexico which supports a distinct caste system, the organizational hierarchies are highly defined and formal. One is expected to "go through the appropriate channels" for approvals and the ultimate decision rests at the top of the organization. On the other hand, the people have a "godfather" system in which a wealthier relative or family friend cares for the needs of those in his charge—which sometimes is the whole village in the rural areas. Thus, although this concept of sharing to take care of those less fortunate is often associated with the communist/socialist movements, it is more likely traceable to the ancient caste systems. This seems probable since the value of Community certainly outlasted the communist movements in Latin America.

Similarly, one can begin to trace the origins of the values of Efficiency and Quality of Life. As we recall the Puritan work ethic in early New England, we can imagine the value of Efficiency—of earning a living, making things work well, improving tools etc. until finally moving into the Industrial Age—having a strong influence over the value of Quality of Life. On the other hand, the indigenous peoples of the Americas had lived off the land and learned to appreciate the natural world over the need for industrial advancement. Today, the different emphasis placed on these two values still create long debates in governments, not to mention around many kitchen tables. Consider the tremendous effort made by the environmental groups to ensure that the requirement for environmental protection standards and clean-up measures were inserted into the NAFTA—a trade agreement designed primarily to improve the potential for business.

CULTURE

Cultures are built on the base values of a society. Webster's dictionary describes culture as "a particular human group's mastery of the art of living. Various phases of culture are language, religion, customs, industries, all of which are general social inheritance of the group, which may continue to develop or retrogress independently of all other groups, or may have its culture modified by contact with other cultures." Also, culture is defined as "All the knowledge, crafts, art, literature, beliefs, and customs of a people."[1] Geert Hofstede, in his seminal work on culture, states, "culture is the collective programming of the mind which distinguishes the members of one human group from another.—Culture could be defined as the interactive aggregate of common characteristics that influence a human group's response to its environment.—Culture, in this sense, includes systems of values; and values are among the building blocks of culture."[2]

Edward Hall's study of cultures, beginning in the 1950's, looked at the very basic, personal implications of cultural backgrounds. For instance, he shows that culture impacts the human sensory values. How one perceives the sense of space is culturally biased. Different peoples view what is aesthetic, what is particularly pleasing, what is uncomfortable, etc. differently. To identify some of the various ways people think of the use of space, consider, for instance, the design of a Japanese garden. The total space used for the garden may be very compact, yet the visual perception often is one of vastness. A path through the garden frequently will be irregular and even suddenly interrupted, causing the person to move slowly or completely stop and view the surroundings—to experience the spatial environment. In Western cultures, paths are normally as straight as possible to provide the shortest and most efficient route. In a Western garden, one will often find a criss-crossed pattern of straight paths providing the visitor the quickest route to the section of the garden the person wants to view. Sometimes, you may discover a circular or arched path offering a broader view and more aesthetic look. If this is in a public garden, look for the worn make-shift path people have developed to short cut the longer circular walk.

In societies less individualistic than the U.S., such as the high context societies in Latin America identified by Hofstede, the use of space is often used to draw people together. Frequently in such countries, cities and towns are centered around the town square or central park. Chapultepec Park in Mexico City is a thriving center of activity in the heart of the city where families gather to meet friends and acquaintances. Village squares are the central places for festivals and holiday gatherings as well as simply casual meeting places. On the other hand, when one considers modern cities in the United States, the square sections and straight efficient streets point to the cultural use of space. As Hall points out, straight streets and corners encroach the least on individual yards and provide the most efficient route for movement and transportation of people who have little need for interaction with other people along the way.

Hall's work further explored the more subtle elements of culture—the aspects that one often attributes more to personalities than cultural learning. Yet culture helps mold personalities. For example, Western cultures place importance on logical, linear thinking. Clear cause and effect logic, developed in the time of Socrates, is used in teaching everything from mathematics to cooking. Most people of Western culture cannot imagine another way to arrive at conclusions. Other cultures are based on a more integrative way of thinking. Rather than separating a problem into its components and solving each part to complete the whole, they will tend toward a more holistic, systemic thought process. Which aspect of the problem is considered in which sequence is not as important as being able to understand the interdependencies of the whole. Examples of such differences can be seen in contract negotiations, for instance. To develop a contract, U.S. negotiators will have listed all of the important points for consideration and tend to bring each to a conclusion in a logical sequence. Mexican negotiators will tend to "jump all around" the issues, talking of many aspects all at once, bounce back and forth between the various issues and eventually reach an agreement on the whole contract. When the two different cultures come together to create a contract with each other, one can imagine the level of frustration of each negotiator.

The manner in which people interact with each other is also impacted by cultural background. Whether a person is gregarious and outgoing or more private and solitary is certainly an aspect of the person's personality. However, how that personality aspect is manifested is culturally influenced. In high context cultures such as in Mexico, people are more involved with each other. This does not mean that people divulge their personal lives to strangers or spend all their time chatting about their neighbors. They are typically very private about their personal lives. However, it does mean that they will tend to be more concerned with "who" than with "what". The manner of communications of a message is equally or more important than the message itself. Politeness is of critical importance. Even a reprimand from a supervisor is delivered without humiliating the person being reprimanded. The message may be loud and vehement, but it will be carefully delivered so as not to offend or humiliate the recipient. The language itself is structured in a way to avoid direct affronts. For example, an English translation of a Spanish phrase would tend to come out something like, "When Mary opened the refrigerator, the milk spilled itself." Note that Mary did not spill the milk.

In a low context, more individualistic, and efficiency oriented society such as the U.S., the emphasis is placed on ensuring that the message is delivered correctly. Content, clarity, and directness are more important than politeness. People in the U.S. tend to separate themselves from the problem or issue so that a reprimand concerning an issue is typically not intended or taken personally. People who have worked in both countries have indicated that in the U.S., people often relish the opportunity to prove their individual ingenuity by identifying and solving problems; whereas, in Mexico, people do not want to identify a problem in their area of responsibility because it is taken as a personal failure. In Mexican culture, a problem that occurs is due to fate and will be fixed; it is not something that can be avoided. Again, the subtly of such a cultural difference is often hard to distinguish. Typically, a U.S. supervisor who is unaware of the distinction will simply not understand why no one told him about a potential issue before it occurred when it appears that it was obvious to the Mexican employees. It requires excellent cultural sensitivity to learn to ask the right questions the right way to gain the information that must be shared between people of different cultural backgrounds.

Hall describes other subtle cultural aspects of people that are often overlooked as personality traits. He mentions that even motion is based in culture. Hall tells that studies have shown that new-born infants tend to move in very similar manners. Older children and adults, however, assume a rhythm in their movements that matches the movements of other people in the same culture. Thus, how one walks, sits, and simply moves will be different than how a person in a different culture moves. In many cases, two people from very different cultures become annoyed with each other, but they cannot actually identify what was annoying. It can be something as subtle as the fact they are simply "out of rhythm". When people are working with each other on a regular basis, it is often these deep seated, subtle cultural differences that create the tensions that occur. Usually, people will accept another's customs and often enjoy learning about them. However, the almost imperceptible cultural differences can make working together difficult when the people are unaware of them.

A key element of culture that is too often minimized as a difference is the language of the people. Since English is recognized as the universal language of business, many native English speaking people, especially in the U.S., assume it is unnecessary to learn the native language of the other culture. Although it is true that many business transactions can be conducted in English, and translators can assist in most negotiations, it is critical to learn the language if one expects to establish a long-term relationship. Learning the way ideas and concepts are expressed in a different language begins to help one understand some of the cultural subtleties described above. Noting the words that do not exist in a different language also provides insight into the culture and values of a people. Further, and perhaps most important, attempting to learn the language of the people of another culture indicates a true interest in and respect for that people. An attempt to communicate with people in their way is usually appreciated.

Geert Hofstede's studies of cultural differences are more closely related to the business environment than most. In an in-depth study of employees of a multinational corporation, Hofstede noted the differences of people from different cultures who had the same positions in the company. In this way, since the general position in the hierarchy, the typical responsibilities, and the general level of education were the same, the key differences he studied were primarily based in culture.

Hofstede categorized four primary behavioral aspects of culture: the Power Distance Index; Uncertainty Avoidance; Individualism; and Masculinity. In his book, *Culture's Consequences*, Hofstede hypothesizes the historic causes of the differences among cultures on the scale of the four aspects; however, more important, he begins to predict certain behaviors of people based on where the specific culture fits on the scale. For example, in cultures with a very high level of Power Distance, one should expect a formal hierarchical structure both in the public society as well as in organizations. In such cultures, people in business organizations tend to follow strict guidelines relating to who is entitled to make decisions, who speaks to whom, and even where people are seated in a meeting room. The position of "boss" may be envied, respected, and resented. On a societal level, cultures with an extremely high Power Distance Index may tend to be volatile since the top levels that control the power cannot be easily negotiated or challenged. There is seldom a means of discussing issues among the various levels. Thus, when the populace is upset with the top level, a coup or revolution takes place to change the power control.

Cultures with a high Individualism index tend to experience an entrepreneurial business environment. Even within large organizations, people tend to look for ways to make their own decisions or at least significantly influence decisions made. Employees will be more prone to managing their own careers and more likely to move from organization to organization to enhance their own individual positions. The highest levels of concern and interests center around the individual and that person's immediate family. On a societal level, there is usually no formal caste system recognized since it is expected that all individuals should take care of themselves. Thus, it is proposed that each person has both the opportunity and responsibility to enhance their social and economic position. Although too often the social system is structured to make such opportunity more difficult for people in certain groups to obtain, when an individual does move ahead it is more easily accepted than in societies with low Individualism indices.

Hofstede further points out that cultures that have a high Uncertainty Avoidance index will tend to be more "rule oriented". Whether rules are actually documented or not, employees will prefer to have very clear guidelines as to what is expected and how they should perform their tasks. Changing the norm in such cultures is difficult since people will need a clear understanding of why the usual way of doing something should be changed. They will need to be convinced that the new way proposed will work and will be better since risk is typically avoided in these cultures. People in cultures that have a low Uncertainty Avoidance index will tend to be more comfortable with broad guidelines describing positions in an organization or tasks to be done. They are more likely to make plans for an unknown future with the expectation that things may change and plans will be altered. On a societal level, high Uncertainty Avoidance cultures will be less tolerant of new trends and deviant social groups that live outside the social norms.

Hofstede's masculinity index measures the importance that a culture puts on assertiveness and domination versus cooperation and nurturing. Although it would seem that high Masculinity would correspond to high Individualism, that is not necessarily so. High Masculinity tends to indicate such things as distinct gender roles, a desire for material wealth to indicate position, and expectation that a nurturing role be played by women in the society. High Masculinity and lower Individualism would indicate that people still tend to group themselves, but that mixed gender groups are unlikely.

Although one may disagree with precisely the position Hofstede gives each studied culture on the four aspect scales, a valuable lesson can be learned by observing the various positions of different cultures / countries on the scales. When thinking of NAFTA (North American Free Trade Agreement), we tend to think of a virtually borderless business community between the United States and its two neighbors, Canada and Mexico. The trade agreement greatly simplifies laws and tariffs that regulate moving products and services among the three countries. However, when we review the positions of these three countries on Hofstede's culture scales, we can see that conducting business among the three will be quite different from one to another. On the scale of Power Distance and Uncertainty Avoidance, both Canada and the United States are very close together—both on the low ends, while Mexico is the polar opposite. On the scale of Masculinity, Mexico is at the very high end, the U.S. is towards the high end, and Canada moves to the lower end. On the scale of Individualism, the United States reaches the extreme high end and Mexico is at the very low end, while Canada comes out closer to the U.S. but not as extreme. As we consider the implications of these differences that Hofstede's study indicate, we can predict that many business people used to operating in a particular manner in their own country or with one of the other countries will be very surprised as they expand their business across the whole trade bloc. Methods that worked well before will suddenly need to be changed. Cultural understanding and sensitivity will become critical to business success.

CUSTOMS

According to Webster's, a custom is a common usage or practice carrying the authority of long standing and public acceptance. The example given is the sending of Christmas cards. Everyone can easily identify many customs from their own cultural backgrounds. They tend to encompass everything from style of dress, to mode of greetings, to favorite foods, to holiday celebrations, to style of dance. In business, for example, most U.S. business people have now learned that presenting business cards with the name facing the recipient is an important custom in Japan.

Customs are the most easily changed aspect of cultures. "Cultural borrowing" that is often discussed and sometimes feared usually refers to the change in customs observed when people of one country interact with those of another. The world wide acceptance of blue jeans as casual clothing and Coca-Cola as a common beverage are examples of such cultural borrowing. Similarly, the rapid growth in the number of Sushi restaurants in the U.S. is an indication of the influence of Japanese business during the 1980's. The United States is often accused of cultural "imperialism" as corporations move into another country and people begin adopting the use of U.S. products. However, although customs tend to be altered fairly easily, the more deep-seated aspects of culture previously discussed change very slowly over centuries, and the core values that anchor a culture almost never change.

It is important for corporations to identify all three aspects of a new market—the customs, the culture, and the values. Further, they need to consciously decide whether or not they want to alter products and strategies to conform to all three aspects, or play the role of "change agent" and introduce new products, services, and methods of doing things. In either case, they need to recognize that customs may be easily altered, cultures may tolerate new ideas, but core values must be honored and respected.

All aspects of the new market are important in marketing strategies and product designs. A company may decide to produce a product or service that meets the requirements of a unique culture and target that specific country, or to produce something that meets a smaller niche in a specific culture but appeals to the same niche in many cultures. When the function and visual attractiveness of the product, the package, the promotional literature and advertising are developed, the various aspects of customs, culture, and values must be taken into consideration.

OPERATIONS

Once a corporation has decided to enter a new country market, the question of how to operate in that market arises. Whose customs and cultural aspects should the company follow? If a company is strictly regulated in its own country, there may be a desire to move to another country where the regulations are less restricted. It is simple to think of such examples in the United States. Consider the environmental and safety restrictions to which oil refineries must comply versus how similar refineries are allowed to function in other parts of the world.

Similarly, if there is a "custom" of side-payments and extra favors in return for easing of bureaucratic procedures or granting of contracts, does a corporation whose home country does not permit such activities need to follow the custom? Is the corporation that meets its home country's laws and regulations at a competitive disadvantage when it tries to operate in a country where other companies are not so restricted? Perhaps a more difficult situation to consider occurs when a company enters a culture that operates with a strictly defined caste system. In such a culture, it is not uncommon to find that people receive positions and salaries based on who their relatives are or where they were born, rather than on their aptitude and talents. Yet, to change the structure may result in chaos and resentment among all of the employees who have grown up used to a certain hierarchy.

Product and service issues often arise in new countries pertaining to custom and culture as well. For example, if a product is a new concept to a market, to what extent is the education of the market to the correct use of the product the responsibility of the manufacturer, the distributor, or the user? A well known example of the issue is the use of pesticides in third world countries. With appropriate use, the pesticides could be a major boon to the country, increasing agricultural output to gain all of the associated benefits . However, without proper education, the misuse of the product can, and in some situations has, become deadly. Educating a massive population is very costly, and not the custom in the country. Who needs to take the responsibility. Too often, a company's unofficial response to such issues follows the old adage, "When in Rome, do as the Romans." This indecisive attitude, however, will typically lead to major problems and difficulties in maintaining operations in the new country.

Richard T. DeGeorge at the University of Kansas has proposed a seemingly simple guideline to help a corporation answer such questions. Dr. DeGeorge advises that companies operate consistently with integrity. Establishing policies and making decisions are simplified for all employees when the corporation historically bases all of its operations on basic integrity. To quote Dr. DeGeorge, "Acting with integrity means both acting in accordance with one's highest self accepted norms of behavior and imposing on oneself the norms demanded by ethics and morality. Since the word *integrity* implies self-imposed norms, a demand that companies act with integrity is more acceptable and less threatening to many multinationals than is a demand that they act ethically or morally—even though the two amount to the same demand."[3]

DeGeorge emphasizes that an important aspect of this operating principle is consistency. A company cannot alter its mode of behavior for each country and culture in which it functions. The sheer practicality of managing many different rules and policies prohibits such variability. More important, however, consistency greatly facilitates strategic and operating decisions for employees wherever they are located. For one reason, if the employees recognize consistent application of policies across the organization, they will know what is expected in a given situation. Also, the employees will tend to believe they themselves will be treated consistently upon making a decision. Further, a corporation that has a solid reputation of operating with integrity will find that its employees are less likely to be put in a potentially compromising situation in the first place since others already know how the corporation will respond. For example, according to Dr. DeGeorge, IBM is known throughout the world as a corporation that will neither take nor give bribes. Consequently, IBM employees are almost never in the position where they would have to decide whether to comply with the "customary" request for extraordinary payments.

Many of the examples Dr. DeGeorge provides point to the fact that sometimes operating with integrity without putting the company at a competitive disadvantage requires empathy and imagination coupled with common sense. He provides two examples of "side-payments" that illustrate the point. In one case, a trucker is at the border to deliver a load of fresh butter. He is directed to pull to the side. As he waits, he sees other truckers paying a slight fee and going directly through. Knowing his instructions are to not pay bribes, the trucker waits. Four hours later, he notices the now melted butter dripping out from the truck's door. In such a case, perhaps the trucker would be better off to pay the relatively nominal payment, proceed with his delivery, and immediately report the situation to his company so that it could be dealt with at a higher level in both the company and the government. On the other hand, three competing companies placed very large orders for silk needed for their products. All three were told the silk was back-ordered and would be delayed three to six months. Soon, one company's purchasing agent received an anonymous call that explained the silk could be delivered immediately for a silent payment of $100,000 more. The agent paid the money and got delivery. The second company's purchasing agent placed a call to a government "friend" and offered $100,000 for delivery of the order. That company also received delivery. The third company did not pay additional money and received its delivery in six months. Were the other two wrong? Absolutely. Was the third company at a competitive disadvantage? Absolutely. Was there anything else that could be done?

In the latter case, it was pointed out that often ingenuity and moral courage are required to operate in new markets. The situation involving the silk needed both. The original orders did not reflect the true market price of the silk. Apparently, it was under priced by at least $100,000; and therefore, the manufacturing company was not profiting as it could have from the transactions. The third company might have been able to openly approach the manufacturing company and re-initiate the bidding, offering to openly pay $100,000 more for the initial order. The other two companies could match the offer or bid even more if the market demanded it. In this way, the $100,000 would be recognized as direct cost of goods; the manufacturer would be the only beneficiary of the market demand; and the third company would have demonstrated that it intended to operate openly and honestly with all parties involved. It is not an easy or quick solution to the problem; but perhaps it is one that will provide the best long term results.

Why should a corporation be expected to take such drastic steps? Often, companies do not want to attract attention or publicity, or become involved in the quagmire of local politics and corruption. Nevertheless, large corporations desiring to do business in other country markets do have responsibilities beyond those expected of them in their own homeland—especially if they are dealing with emerging markets and third world countries. Dr. DeGeorge has developed seven norms for operating internationally. They are offered here for consideration:

1. Multinationals should do no intentional direct harm.

2. Multinationals should produce more good than harm for the host country.

3. Multinationals should contribute by their activity to the host country's development.

4. Multinationals should respect the human rights of their employees.

5. To the extent that local culture does not violate ethical norms, multinationals should respect the local culture and work with and not against it.

6. Multinationals should pay their fair share of taxes.

7. Multinationals should cooperate with the local government in developing and enforcing just background institutions. [Background institutions include private and government institutions that guarantee fair competition, protect human rights, conserve the country's resources, etc.][4]

Given the challenges presented in identifying and understanding a society's values, culture, and customs and then operating in such a way as to support them with consistent integrity, the big "C" of Culture may be the most critical element of the marketing strategy that the international marketer has to consider.

NOTES

1. *Webster's Unified Dictionary and Encyclopedia;* H.S. Stuttman Co. Inc., New York, N.Y.; 1959. p. 1092.

2. Hofstede, Geert; *Culture's Consequences—International Differences in Work-Related Values, Vol. 5*; Sage Publications, England & California; 1984.p. 18-21.

3. DeGeorge, Richard T.; *Competing with Integrity in International Business*; Oxford University Press; New York & Oxford; 1993. p. 6.

4. Ibid.: p. 42-56.

A Marketing Planning Scenario

PREFACE

The following section provides a pragmatic example of developing a marketing plan in a transnational environment while considering some of the implications of the use of information communications technologies. It also brings to life some of the situations and the potential for changes to strategies that occur because of cultural differences. The company and the characters are fictitious, but the anecdotes are based on the true experiences of professionals who have been working in the described environment.

The scenario is based on the development of a marketing plan for taking an information communications product into the business to business market in Mexico. It will raise the questions that need to be considered in any transnational marketing strategy, but will provide potential solutions from the perspective of doing business in the Mexican culture. As previously mentioned, it is recognized that there is no single "correct" answer for the development of a marketing strategy. The hope here is that the scenario will raise the questions and potential issues and provide some possible direction that can be discussed and considered for its applicability by the marketing practitioner or student in their own situation.

As the readers go through the scenario, they will discover aspects of Mexican culture and values that impact marketing strategies. They will also be given the opportunity to consider the use of information communications technologies in the development and implementation of marketing strategies. The scenario format is used to help readers relate the information to a real situation, and to consequently, make it more memorable. When the readers are faced with a similar situation, they will hopefully find that they have had the opportunity to think through potential solutions and outcomes in a holistic manner based on having worked through this simulated plan.

INTRODUCTION: CARLSBAD EQUIPMENT COMPANY

Carlsbad Equipment Company is a manufacturer of data communications equipment products. Its headquarters is located in the new office/retail park on the north edge of Phoenix, Arizona. Employing almost 8000 people, Carlsbad Equipment has two manufacturing plants—the original just outside of Tempe, and a relatively new plant on highway 80 in Bisbee. Although the recent fiscal year revenue results of $840 million were positively received by Carlsbad's bank creditors and the stock market, senior management took them as an initiative to begin serious planning discussions. The $840 million was still showing growth, 9% over the previous year; but it made this the second consecutive year that the growth rate had declined. Since the year had been quite profitable with a net of $130 million, the planning discussions were definitely up-beat. Management had decided to look for new markets for their products to prolong the growth rate.

Thus, with a clear mission of finding new markets to sustain at least a 10%/ year growth rate, and knowledge that the U.S. market on both the west coast and east coast were already heavily penetrated by Carlsbad Equipment company's key competitors located on the coasts, the strategic marketing task team looked toward Mexico. It appeared to be the most logical target given Mexico's expected economic growth, the company's proximity to the Mexican border—68 miles from Agua Prieta in Sonora to the CE plant in Bisbee-, and the anticipated need for data communications equipment as Mexico upgrades its communications infrastructure. Further, with the passage of the North American Free Trade Agreement, Carlsbad Equipment could be price competitive in the Mexican market. Therefore, with the next market having been selected as Mexico, the team was now about to develop a marketing plan for doing business in Mexico.

[At the senior management meeting at the headquarters of Carlsbad Equipment Company]—"so you can see with what has been presented,—with a saturated U.S. market and at least a year before our newest breakthrough product reaches the volume we need to sustain our targeted rate of growth, Mexico and potentially other countries in South America are critical markets for us. We have selected one of our finest marketers to head down there and figure out how to get things started. Phil Sierra is the right guy to jump-start this project. He has been very successful in introducing the GCB model into the product family this past year. The GCB is now positioned to be at break-even before the end of this fiscal, so I think we can safely ask Phil to leave that to the others and move on to our newest challenge. With Phil in the lead, we can expect big things to happen quickly!"

Phil Sierra has been with Carlsbad Equipment Company for nine years in increasingly responsible positions. He started with Carlsbad Equipment as the manager of distribution in the Southwest region, having worked as a salesman in one of the distributors in Tucson. From distribution, through customer service, Phil had spent some time in product marketing which he thoroughly enjoyed. Most recently, he was the team leader for the new product introduction group established to develop the GCB. The team had successfully launched the product from design to full manufacturing in 20 months, and Phil had received special recognition at the annual sales meeting as the "father of GCB". A self-described "Type A" personality, Phil is a very hard-working, forthright, honest individual; a graduate of the Air Force Academy; and a manager that people genuinely like to work for. He demands near perfection from everyone he works with, but is considered fair and reasonable by those in his department. Phil has gladly accepted the Mexican assignment and is anxious to get started.

Phil's first task is to recruit three co-workers to assist in building the business plan. He has chosen Joseph Tricot, currently in product marketing for the AAB, the most well known product from Carlsbad Equipment. Joseph's background has mostly been in the law department, and Phil felt that would be a strength needed on the team for business analyses, distributor arrangements, and understanding trade requirements. Phil's second recruit, Bob Washington, is an old colleague from the Air Force academy, and another "Type A" personality. Phil knows he can count on Bob to push through any obstacles the team might encounter in trying to get this project going. The third person is Marlena Albright. Marlena has a strong background in marketing and some international experience from her college days. Her school had a students-abroad program in which selected students spent one year at the University of Hamburg in Germany to learn international business as well as the cultural impact of foreign business in a country.

This is the team that will develop the business case for Carlsbad Equipment company's entry into Mexico. Their recommendations will be presented to the senior management group for consideration and action.

CHAPTER 4

The Chicken or the Egg; Which Comes First, Product or Market Definition?

"Which products are we going to introduce into Mexico, Phil? All of them or one at a time?" Bob Washington was anxious to get the team started and was trying to size the scope of the task based on the number of products involved.

"We can't know which products—if any—until we assess what market exists in Mexico, Bob. There is always the possibility that we will need a whole new product to meet the market requirements. Our overall goal is to sustain Carlsbad *company* revenue growth, not a particular product growth. Our first task is to define our market and identify customer characteristics and needs." The urgency in Marlena's voice indicated that she also was anxious to get started, but she was concerned that the whole task force would be taken down a technology path and forget about market requirements. Carlsbad Equipment was known for high quality technology, but had traditionally been in the position of finding customers that needed their products rather than finding the product their customers wanted.

"But we have to know what we are starting with before we can identify the market. After all, we can't just build anything in the line of data communications. I understood that we are supposed to move existing product into the Mexican market, so we have to decide which product we are going to sell."

"Of course, you are both right. We are going to work with our current product line to open the market, Bob. But that doesn't mean that we can't add some functionality or change the packaging or something if the market requirements call for it. Also, we need to consider the long term and determine if there is a demand for a product we don't have yet, but could develop relatively easily. So, Marlena, we do have to identify the market, the customers, the requirements, and the potential. However, we can narrow our research to identify the market that best fits our current product line. After all, if there is a need for the product or products as they are right now, without changing anything, our costs could be minimized, and we would be ready to start selling right away. Since we have an existing line, it is different than if we were designing a new product or company from scratch." Phil was planning the team's efforts as he was speaking. "We will have to research both product fit and market need simultaneously, and look at the whole picture together rather than consider each issue separately. So, I think I can see how we can start to utilize each of the talents of this illustrious group. We'll figure out what we have to know together, then each one can research the area according to his or her expertise. We'll get back together and see how it all fits—which product in which market."

The team identified product and market questions for nearly two weeks. The first step was to identify the features, functions, and specifications of the AAB product—the one that was currently selling the best in the United States—as well as the new GCB model. The questions that arose as they considered the product included:

What infrastructure interfaces are needed in Mexico?

For example, are electrical plugs everywhere in Mexico the same as in the U.S. ? What are the specifications on the coax cable used there? Are the communications jacks the same as in the U.S.? Are surge protectors commonly used to protect communications equipment or is that something that will need to be packaged along with the product?

What are the networking requirements of the product?

Does it require conditioned communications lines or can it adjust to some amount of "noise" on the line? What speeds and protocols can be supported? Which network media are supported—copper, fiber, wireless?

Do the products meet the legal standards in Mexico that must be met?

Standards can include performance, quality, and even labeling. What are the packaging requirements for this type of product, i.e. showing type of product and origin in Spanish on the outside of the box?

What functions and features of the products could easily be altered for Spanish speaking users? What is the user documentation like?

Will the administration and maintenance procedures have to be altered for use in Mexico?

For example, how will "800" type of customer service be offered in Mexico? Also, how will customer service be handled for Spanish speaking customers, and possibly distributors?

Joseph was particularly interested in the software protection that might be built into the product. The NAFTA has specific provisions to protect intellectual property rights, and the Mexican government had given all indications that they intend to stand behind those provisions. However, protecting software from being copied for "sharing" or for counterfeiting is even difficult in the U.S. where people are fully aware of the laws. He wondered if special precautions would be needed in Mexico where the media has not made such an issue of the inappropriateness of "sharing" software.

The team identified numerous questions regarding the target market as well. Some of them included:

- Are the growth industries in Mexico the same as the ones identified in the U.S.? What is the relative size of company in the industries targeted? How many companies are there in the target industry? Where are the geographic concentrations, if any?

- What is the estimated potential for data communications in the near term? in the long run?

- Are the benefits of using the products as identified by the U.S. customers also valued in Mexico? By the same type of customer?

- What are the functions that are required in Mexico for data communications? How would a customer likely use a data communications product? Where would they likely want the product to be placed—in a computer room, in an electrical closet, in plain view; and consequently would that change its physical appearance? Are there unique environmental conditions such as very high or low humidity?

After considerable research, phone calls, and personal visits, the team reconvened to consider the findings.

Marlena walked in wearing a huge grin, "Wow! This general market information is really exciting! Even the research assistant in our library started getting into it. At first, he didn't think much of this project because he figured that Mexico was so far behind in data communications that trying to identify and quantify a market would be futile. Boy!—not true. Wait till you see what we've found."

"Hey, great!" Joe was grinning too. "That's good to hear because as near as we can tell, Carlsbad has equipment to sell in Mexico, too. We need a few minor adjustments and some "physical appearance" alterations, but functionally the products should work just fine."

"Well, let's get started. Marlena, why don't you begin with what you've discovered." Phil and the others settled in to take notes.

"OK. Well, first—looking at industries in Mexico, we found that many companies are owned by or affiliated with large conglomerates. Most of those are called 'Grupo—whatever'. For instance, Grupo Pulsar owns tobacco and insurance companies. Grupo ICA is the largest construction and engineering firm. Grupo VISA owns companies in beverages, financial services, and banking—they bought the second largest bank in Mexico, Bancomer. A lot of these Grupos have a long history of one family in Mexico that accumulated the companies and built the conglomerates. Consequently, in some of the cases, the companies in a Grupo are strongly tied—philosophically, so to speak—for instance, such as who they will do business with.

"On the other hand, there are many small companies in Mexico— highly concentrated in Mexico city—that are just as anxious to utilize more communications technologies as the big guys.— And, a lot of companies are affiliating with, or partnering with, or even merging with U.S. companies right now. Those companies are looking to their U.S. partners to bring in the technical expertise as well as some of the capital required to invest in technologies. For instance, CIFRA, a retail conglomerate in Mexico, controls five major Mexican retail supermarket and restaurant chains, operating over 200 stores. It turns out that Wal-mart owns 49% of CIFRA. And as for data comm, CIFRA supports point of sale transactions in many of their stores and connects them to the major bank networks to check credit, avoid credit card fraud, etc. More than 150 of their stores are on the CIFRA proprietary X.25 network! According to this terrific report we found from Pyramid Research in Massachusetts, CIFRA is applying to the Mexican SCT , the Secretaria de Comunicaciones y Transportaciones, to be allowed to provide services over their network. One of the applications they want to offer is to enable Mexicans in the U.S. to wire transfer money to their family in Mexico; and then, the person in Mexico picks up their cash in the closest CIFRA owned store. What a great way to pull in retail traffic, don't you think?"

"It sure is. It all sounds interesting—but can you help us relate all of this information to Carlsbad Equipment products?" Joe had been fascinated with the discussion but kept trying to narrow the focus to product sales in his mind.

"Oh yeah—of course. Well, key point is that the Mexican data communications market is not unsophisticated as some people thought. Based on the subscription information from Information Week, Data Communications magazine, the Wall Street Journal, etc., the people in Mexico are reading the same information and seeing the same ads as our customers here in the States. The good news is that the market is far from saturated, and the people are fairly anxious to enhance their technology use—of course, it is has to be with the right product and price.

"The high potential industries align pretty closely with traditional data comm users in the States. The banks were the first to see the need for data networking; and the big ones built their own networks. The predictions are that banking and financial services will be upgrading their networks to higher speed transmissions and more applications. Right now, the banking industry in Mexico is in a state of 'discontinuity' so to speak. With the industry being opened to foreign competition now, some of the banks may take on U.S. partners, and all of them will have to get much more efficient to compete with the big, already established international banks. The banks recognize that they need more automation and networking to effectively and profitably compete—especially if Mexico can keep a cap on inflation. In the old days, banks didn't have to worry about foreign competition, and they could make a handsome profit just based on tremendous rates of inflation. They know those days are over. The banking service offerings are getting updated too. For instance, checking accounts as we know them have only been offered to the general public in Mexico in the last five or so years. Most everyday purchases and transactions have traditionally been in cash. So you can see the growing need for data communications there.

"The large manufacturing and process companies are also good prospects for enhanced data networking. CEMEX, the huge international cement company has the most advanced private network outside the banking sector. Celanese Mexicana, the conglomerate that has chemical and fiber producers, will likely upgrade their data comm to have better communications back to their U.S. partner, DuPont.

"Another good sector to consider is the government utilities and transportation companies. They may take a little longer to penetrate and sell—like government accounts in the U.S.—but they are pretty advanced in the use of data communications. For example, the electric company, the CFE—Comision Federal de Electricidad—has some areas where there network automatically sends a message to report broken lines or power surges. They even have sections in Mexico City where the electric meters transmit each day's data to a central computer to track and bill for usage. I am sure that they are planning to expand their data comm even more because, according to Pyramid's report, the CFE is planning to sell their right of way to network providers for fiber optic paths—but the requirement is that 1 fiber of each cable will be reserved for CFE's use.

"So, at least on this first round, my recommendation is that we start qualifying specific prospects in banking and the financial services, the medium and large manufacturing companies with multiple sites, and begin working on specific government customers for the longer term. We will need to find a way to identify specific companies, the decision makers in those companies, and then do our homework on what they already have, what they need, how they buy—and from whom, etc. You know—the *real* research. I plan to first check our current customer base and see which ones have subsidiaries, affiliates, or partners in Mexico. Can you guys help me identify other sources of info?"

"We will all be trying to find more sources as we keep going through this, that's for sure. Looks like you have a pretty good start, though. Let me talk a little about what Joe and I discovered about the infrastructure the products need to work into." Bob and Joe had tried to determine what kind of networking capacity and capabilities were available in Mexico. They also had conducted a function and feature inventory on the AAB and GCB models to determine if any major changes would have to be made to the products to functionally fit into the Mexican market.

"Things certainly are in a state of major change there—but it looks as if it is changing in a really positive way for Carlsbad Equipment products. So far, as Marlena pointed out, a lot of the data communications networks have been private networks, although there is a government owned TELEPAC packet switched network. Most of the private networks have been satellite based because service over the local connections from the business site to the network either wasn't available or wasn't good quality. Now, with competition moving in, the prediction is that in the near future, the VSAT networks will be relegated to back up facilities, and advanced data networking capacity will be available. As a matter of fact, according to that same Pyramid report that Marlena referred to, Telmex just initiated a new program called 'Fiber to the Business' that will connect almost a 150 Mexican businesses to an advanced services network. They will offer remote terminals for business connected to public switches via fiber optics for high quality digital links between offices or buildings. They pretty much had to upgrade their offerings because with the partnerships occurring—like MCI and Banamex, the largest private banking network in Mexico—the competition is going to get intense as soon as Telmex's monopoly agreement expires at the beginning of 1997. The good news here is that the network upgrades that are being predicted in the next 2-5 years are all the state-of-the-art communications media and protocols that we have been working on for the U.S. "

Bob's report spawned a thought with Phil. "Bob, you mentioned the Telmex monopoly agreement. How political do you think this environment is?"

"Well, that is a question we will have to check out as we go forward. The head of the SCT is a government appointee, but the staff people are permanent career employees. The federal government does still own part of Telmex and the TELEPAC packet switched network, so they are certainly a potential customer for us—and maybe a distributor, I don't know yet. But, we do know that since there just was a presidential election, the players should be pretty much the same for awhile. The president has a single six year term, so I expect that his appointees serve the term with him. However, according to the U. S.

newspapers and analysts, the new President will have to keep his pledge to break up the "old-boy" network that has been in charge of everything for a long time. People have indicated that as the Mexican system opens to more of a two party system things will be a little confusing. Vendors like us will have to be doubly careful to qualify the person we are dealing with to be certain they are authorized to negotiate contracts. It appears a little more difficult than selling to the U.S. government where you can at least you know whom you need to talk to.

"The change in the Telmex monopolistic structure will impact the market regarding the pricing structure. The cost of network capacity that our potential customers will have to pay will change—the question is, will it go up or down? Looking again at the Pyramid Research report, installation of business lines used to be subsidized across other services. Telmex anticipates a rise in packet data services as they more closely align cost to services—but on the other hand, as the market opens and the ' partnership' networks begin competing prices should go down. As we look at our pricing, we will need to consider the total systems/service costs to our customers.

"When we considered the specific products themselves, we determined the functionality for data communications will be the same, since the use of the products are basically the same in Mexico as in the U.S. What we might consider, however, is new cabinetry. Many of our potential customers will be in Mexico City, I'm sure; and the air quality there is very poor. Mexico City is one of the most polluted cities in the world. The government recognizes the problem and wants to start fixing it—but it will take years to reverse the trends. For our prod—"

Phil interrupted as he was thinking out loud, "I wonder what made Mexico City so polluted?"

"It really is a combination of many things." Marlena offered. "Historically, the city was built in a valley, on an island in a lake. It was a beautiful location that offered the Aztec Indians shelter and water as well as a defensible position because of the lake. The legend is that a priest told them to settle where they saw the great eagle; and as they entered the valley, they saw an eagle land on a cactus there.-That's the eagle on the Mexican flag.-Then as the country developed and more and more people moved into the city to earn a living, gain an education, enter business, and so on—and more and more trees were cut down and buildings put up—and more and more cars came along—and factories were built, pollution increased. And because of the mountains around the city, on many sultry days, the pollution can't escape so it lingers over the city."

Joe added, "Yeah, with 20 million people in one city, sort of hemmed in with mountains, pollution is pretty hard to avoid. Like Marlena said though, they are beginning to take steps to try to help. People are only allowed to drive their cars on certain days. For example, if you are allocated Monday, Wednesday, and Saturdays as your days to drive, you have to take public transportation the other days. That can be a real hassle if the trains aren't running on time or there is a breakdown at rush hour."

"Eventually, when the infrastructure is more available, that situation should really create a great market for our products." Everyone looked a little puzzled at Bob's comment. "Think about the opportunity for telecommuting! Wouldn't you rather work at home on the days you aren't supposed to drive than spend your time on a crowded train or bus?

"Anyway, Joe and I think we ought to consider environmentally 'hardening' the product's cabinets. Many people in Mexico City keep their windows open, and manufacturing sites are always dustier than office buildings, and with the pollution and all—a closed cabinet with minimum need for venting would provide longer service with less problems. While we are at it, it would be good to make the product as small as possible, too. As you can imagine, at least in Mexico City, space is a premium."

"Another change that we need shouldn't be too costly, but will take time. Our documentation and training manuals all need to be translated into Spanish. And, the shipping cartons have to identify the product and origin in Spanish. We have to consider operational buttons and messages on the machine itself, too. Some of the buttons are already identified with the internationally standardized figures, but a few are in English. I'm not sure yet just what it takes to change those remaining few and to translate the machine messages into Spanish, but I really believe those changes are important. The data communications market is as advanced as in the U.S.—but not as prolific yet. A lot of people will be new users and will need a user—friendly environment— especially in their own language." Joe wanted to ensure the task force allotted enough time to ensure all the details would be taken care of so the products would be ready for the Mexican market. "Pyramid Research indicated that the data communications equipment and the terminals markets in Mexico will double by 1998 over the 1993 numbers. That is certainly significant enough that we want to make sure our products please the users right off the bat. Details are important because we can't afford any bad starts."

"Amen! So, who can meet with documentation about the translation?" Phil jotted down notes and names as Joe volunteered. "Great. Thanks. I will join Bob at the meeting with manufacturing and design to talk about the new cabinets."

"I will take the next step to begin to identify specific customers. Any ideas for additional sources for information?" Marlena reminded the team that they had skipped that part of the discussion.

"Oh, that's right. Let's see, both you and I used the report from Pyramid Research. Arthur Andersen Consulting published a major book last year that describes the impact of the NAFTA on various industries, and identifies more information sources. There are several other private research reports we can purchase, a magazine I just subscribed to called 'Mexico Business', and of course, the other publications' subscriber lists that we use to identify customers in the U.S.—such as 'Information Week', 'Data Communications', etc." Bob was speaking as fast as ideas were coming to him.

Phil was thinking about sources, too. "We can contact the Department of Commerce to get information about exporting to Mexico,—and the World Bank as well. They have a huge library and the research staff has been recommended to me in the past. I'll call the Mexican Consulate also, to see if they can help. And, come to think of it, my cousin works for a large freight forwarder in Houston. I'll give her a call to get some advice from them. They have been working in Mexico for at least six years. I'm sure they have experience they will share.

"Who can concentrate some time to find out about the competition in Mexico? That will need to be a big part of the discussion when we get together next Tuesday."

CHAPTER 5

Competition

"Good morning, Phil—Marlena! Joe just stepped out to grab a cup of coffee. We've been doing some thinking about how we might turn potential competitors in Mexico into partners. I'll wait till Joe gets back and let him talk about the possibility."

"I'm glad to hear you made progress, Bob." Phil sounded a little disappointed. "I tried contacting the World Bank research group. I'm a little confused, actually. I have always heard about the World Bank research library as if you could just walk in and have access to all of this information. I think, if you are actually in Washington, D.C. you can go there—it is called the International Bank for Reconstruction and Development, officially—but you have to request an appointment time, etc. For us here in Phoenix, going there is a little tough. So, I called. I talked to several people in different sections of the Bank's library. All of them were polite, but they told me that they only support the staff of the World Bank and the IMF -International Monetary Fund-. One lady offered to check for me, and if they had a list of data communications companies in Mexico, she would fax it to me. When I called her back, however, she had not found such a list and said she really couldn't do any more since I am not part of the Bank's staff. She referred me to the Main library. When I called there, I got their voice mail directory—I pushed #3 for research requests. That message told me to fax my request and include my fax number. They will notify me if they can help or not, and by when. I haven't gotten an answer yet, but I only sent the request yesterday. It took me three days to get that far."

By now, Joe had returned. "Yeah, I think finding out about the competition will take us a little longer than the four days we allotted. It is definitely different than looking up competitors in the U.S. Here, I get a brochure almost every week advertising a new research report about companies in our industry; and of course, we subscribe to the regular research reports from Datapro and Yankee group. I guess that sort of research just isn't as available about Mexico.

"I did 'empower' myself, though, and spent a little of our money; however, I feel certain that we will all benefit from it before this project is completed. I joined the American Chamber of Commerce of Mexico for Carlsbad Equipment Company."

Marlena started to applaud. "That's terrific, Joe. In my research, just yesterday afternoon I discovered that the American Chamber seemed to have a lot of the information that we will need. I am really glad that you joined."

"It is rather surprising to consider all that is included in a membership that costs less than $600 per year. They publish a magazine called 'Business Mexico', a quarterly report that reviews Mexican trade and industry, and—important for our current search—a membership directory. Besides that, they will provide help and consultation from their International Trade and Investment Department; that includes consultation on commercial regulations, assistance in understanding the NAFTA, and special economic forecasts with analysis of how major issues can affect us. So—"; Joe was pretty proud of his discovery, according to the grin he was wearing. "After I joined, the lady I spoke with in Mexico City said she would fax a listing of member companies that either manufacture or distribute data communications equipment in Mexico. Hopefully, I will receive that list by tomorrow. It will at least give us a start as to which companies we need to know more about as potential competitors."

"This is great! We are starting to find some critical information. My search wasn't totally in vain, either. Besides trying to contact the World Bank, I checked out the Department of Commerce. They have tremendous amounts of information as well as a lot of services I think we will be using as we move forward. They have an on-line research system that provides full text reports on all types of markets in countries. Ha Ha, I spent some of our money too. $5.00 to be exact—to print out a 20 page report at $.25 per page.

"This report was written in July, last year and published by the American Embassy in Mexico City. It indicated that most of the data communications equipment is imported into Mexico from the United

States. Therefore, I concluded that most of the competing equipment we will face will be the same equipment we compete with here. The customers have the same type of local networks as U.S. customers—66% Ethernet, 21% Arcnet, and 13% Token Ring—and we already have a pretty good knowledge of the companies that specialize in interfacing to those.

"The report went on to state, however, that even with the passage of the NAFTA, American companies will face tough competition from Asian companies because many of them started manufacturing operations in Mexico before the NAFTA was in effect. Price is a key differentiator and a way to gain market share, according to this report, and the Asian companies base their strategies on low prices. The other point that came out very clear is that with the current credit crunch making financing very expensive in Mexico, the Japanese and German suppliers have a competitive edge over the American companies because they offer better financing programs. That is something we need to take a very serious look at.

"The good news in the report, however, is that American product is recognized as top quality. Reliability and performance are important as well as a commitment to open system architecture. Just like our customers here, the Mexican companies need equipment that works with multiple vendor networks. Also, product availability is an important factor in the purchasing decision. The report states that not only do customers in Mexico feel an urgency to obtain and use the data equipment, they sort of resent the idea that a company will unfairly benefit from their money if they purchase equipment that isn't immediately available.

"Oh—back to our previous discussion on industry markets—this report certainly verified that banks and financial institutions are the biggest data communications customers, and that the government is also an important target market. However, it indicated that retailers may be a more lucrative market than manufacturing. It didn't give absolute conclusions, but we should probably spend a little time looking at some of the retailers when we do specific company research before locking in on manufacturing, don't you think?—Anyway, I will definitely get back to the Department of Commerce to check for specific companies in the data communications equipment business in Mexico. They have the DOC/Office of Mexico in Washington that has additional resources we can access, either through the field office or calling them directly."

"I think you are absolutely right. Before we conclude on any target market we need to get the best information available. The Pyramid Research report I spoke of last time also indicated a lot of data communications activity in retailing in Mexico." Marlena had also been looking for information on competitors. "I reviewed that report again regarding competition, and it sort of verifies the report you found Phil, that most of the competitors are the ones we know.

Our top three competitors here seem to be already getting established in Mexico. One is distributed by Alcatel which has been doing business in Mexico a very long time. According to the Pyramid report, after privatization, Ericsson which had been a telecom supplier to Mexico for years slipped dramatically because they didn't recognize the need for customer service and quality. Alcatel saw the requirement and became much more productive and competitive. They even established a nation-wide network of service engineers so that they could ensure response to equipment problems within two hours anywhere in the country. Consequently, as they expanded into data communications, they provided our competitor with an established reputation and relationships. That is so important in Mexico that we will have to make a concentrated effort to meet that challenge. Price and availability alone won't do it—customer service is *really* important.

"That particular competitor has other distributors besides Alcatel; and has its own Mexican office too. The sales support and marketing functions are provided by its own office. It seems several companies establish a physical office to provide direct support to their distributors. Some do joint training seminars for customers with the distributor in addition to other joint marketing activities.

"A couple of other of our well known competitors have also entered the Mexican market already. Bancomer, the biggest retail bank, bought 40% of the Mexican operation of our 4th major competitor; and our #2 competitor has struck an alliance with AT&T in Mexico."

"Gosh—are we the last ones in the whole industry to cross the border? I'm beginning to feel awfully late." Bob almost groaned as he immediately began thinking of 'catch-up' ideas.

"Well, we aren't the first at the gate; but we aren't the last either. Anyway, remember what we discovered in the last meeting. This is a long term proposition in a market that is expected to double over five years. The Dept. of Commerce report indicated that over the past couple of years, data equipment imports grew in spite of economic difficulties in Mexico, and is expected to continue in growth. Also, it states that the communications segment leads the developments being adopted by Mexican businesses due to the need for data transfer. The reasons they give for continued growth seem credible to me—more and more businesses are depending on data communications for the operations, and the overall cost of the equipment continues to go down making it more and more affordable. I think we are at the right place at the right time. After all, we are definitely used to competition. It keeps us on the leading edge."

"I think we all agree, Phil. This Pyramid report indirectly points to a lot of upcoming opportunity. For instance, it states that there are 40 licensed Value Added Services -VAS—providers in Mexico, but that most of them are not offering service yet. That will certainly drive more demand for data communications equipment." Marlena then cautioned the team, "We just have to be careful not to panic about being 'late' and make sure our strategy is well thought out, and our products are ready—and available, as Phil pointed out.

"Since we have spent a little money already, why don't we spend a little more and subscribe to a couple of the industry and business publications that our Mexican customers receive? That will help us keep up with the industry position and competitor activity in Mexico."

"That's a good idea—except for one little challenge." Bob had a teasing tone in his comment. "Glancing at this Department of Commerce report Phil brought, it looks as if most of these publications are in Spanish—'PC Magazine in Espanol'; 'Soluciones Avanzadas'; 'RED'. Who here speaks and reads Spanish? Phil, Sierra sounds as if it might be Spanish or Mexican in origin. Any chance that you know the language?"

"Sorry, gang. I'm afraid I don't fit the bill. Sierra sounds Latin, but my father is of Hungarian descent. Way back when my great grandfather came to the United States, he was anxious to fit in so he, and a lot of his friends, 'Americanized' the Hungarian names. My mother is Italian descent; and the little Spanish I learned in high school didn't stick with me since I had no one to practice it with. I'm not the team member who can read the magazines and ads."

"No hay un problema!" It was Marlena who surprised the team. "My family is Mexican. I've spoken Spanish all of my life."

Joe was also surprised. "Albright? What's Mexican about that?"

"That's my married name, remember? My parents moved to Arizona thirty years ago when my father received a scholarship at the university. My two aunts and cousins still live in Mexico—in Hermosillo. I know the language and Mexican culture very well. Actually, I am a little relieved to find out that you didn't know that. I had wondered if I were on this team because of my professional marketing experience, or because of my knowledge of Mexico. I am glad I can offer the team both."

Joe was grinning now. "Boy, so are we. I was beginning to wonder how we were going to complete this strategy if we didn't speak Spanish or understand more about the background of the people who would be our customers. What I have been able to read in this short time so far indicates that it is really critical to be able to speak the language. Even if we don't speak it very well at first, I think the people will appreciate the fact that we are willing to try and to learn. It shows a certain interest and commitment to this venture to try to communicate in the language of Mexico instead of expecting everyone to meet our needs by only speaking English—even though most of the business community speaks English very well, I'm told."

"Things are coming together with this team even better than we expected. I've been trying to read a little about the history of Mexico, too. Perhaps we can set up a whole day and review what each of us has learned about the country—history, geography, politics, economics— whatever. Marlena, if you are willing you could orchestrate the day and fill in the blank spaces the rest of us leave—but I'm not suggesting that you do all the work to teach us. Each of us needs to do our own research and bring the resources we use to share with each other. What do you think?"

Everyone chimed in at once, including Marlena; "That's a good idea, Bob." Phil added, "That will give us a little break from the strictly business view of this project, and broaden our sensitivity and knowledge of Mexico a little. Speaking of a break. Let's take ten minutes now, and then come back to hear about the idea you fellows mentioned of how to turn our potential competition into partners."

"OK—we're back." Joe was gathering his notes to get started. "Here's an idea. Here in the U.S., our equipment has to fit into a network with other vendors equipment to provide the whole service. Whenever Carlsbad gets to do the network design to integrate everything together for the customer, we charge for the time and labor to complete that design—and for the implementation if we are also selected to do that part, right? Well, suppose we give that part up in Mexico, but add more in the U.S. ?"

"What are you getting at, Joe?" Marlena was struggling with the idea of giving up any potential revenue right off the bat upon entering a new market.

"Going back to the Pyramid report," Joe continued, "they identify some systems integrators. One in particular is already targeting the financial industry and doing some business with the government—our potential targets. They already have their own network which they plan to upgrade—making them potential customers. And—they already resell certain types of equipment, including equipment imported from the U.S.—making them both a potential distributor and/ or competitor for us. Suppose we approach them as more than just a distributor—make them a true joint marketing partner. In return for their reselling our equipment into their customer base in Mexico, we contract them to do all the systems integration jobs we get from our U.S. customers who are setting up sites and networks in Mexico. Then, they can do the same. When any Mexican company establishing sites in the U.S. contracts with them, we can be the U.S. 'arm' that actually does the design and implementation."

"What we think is—," Bob jumped in since he had remained silent for about as long as he could stand. "Carlsbad Equipment will need immediate customer contact and credibility in Mexico. What we have discovered today confirms that since so many of our prime competitors are already working there. Strong distributors will give us contact and credibility, but we will still be arm's length away. That makes it more difficult for us to learn about the customers, their requirements, how they are the same or different than our customers here, what's working, and what's not in our marketing strategy. By having at least one partner more closely associated with us, we think we will gain ground faster—and learn the nuances of the market faster, too. If the partner is a marketing partner rather than a real affiliate, Carlsbad Equipment doesn't have to actually put up any cash right away for investment. We give up a little potential revenue by contracting them to do any systems integration work in Mexico, but potentially even gain that back later when they contract us to do the work in the U.S. Besides, instead of having them as a competitor, we get them as a partner. If things work out just terrific, we can always talk about a real joint venture investment-type partnership later. We aren't talking about an exclusive distributorship—we can still have other companies handle our product too. The exclusive would just be in the systems integration jobs.—What do you think?"

Marlena broke the momentary silence. "Actually, I believe that idea has some very good points. When an American company comes into Mexico, it is important to the Mexican businessman that the American company is truly interested in helping him grow his business and be successful. The Mexican businessman really resents an American company that just wants to sell its product, take the money, and move on. He expects and wants a relationship, not just a vendor. An arrangement such as you are describing would create such a relationship—and a good reputation for Carlsbad Equipment. Frankly, it would help us test the degree of commitment of our top management to the market as well. If we can truly support such a joint marketing partnership, and assist in growing the systems integrator's business, Carlsbad Equipment would gain a strong foothold for long term business and profitability in Mexico. I think we should figure out the details for such a proposal."

"I agree. We will have to find out more about this company—you know, all the particulars. Who owns them; are they affiliated with one of the Grupos we already discussed; what is their financial situation; how is their reputation today;—all the things we would need to know if they were to be a joint venture partner in the near future." Phil was thinking of the work to be done for the next meeting. "So, we have a lot to find out. We need more information on the competition.—I'll see if the World Bank research has faxed me anything, and I'll pursue some more of the Department of Commerce reports. Perhaps someone else could check the recent annual reports of our prime competitors and see if they speak about their Latin American, specifically Mexican, strategy. If we are going to face the same companies there as here, we may already have a lot of information on them.

"We need more information about the company you have identified as a potential partner. And—we have to start getting specific information on the customer targets. Well, we're off! "

CHAPTER 6

Customer Targets

"Good morning!" Phil almost shouted the normal greeting as the other team members entered the room.

"Wow! You're certainly 'chipper' this morning. Anything special causing this attitude?" Bob had to chuckle at his old colleague.

"Well, I received some answers from my research requests. The World Bank very politely declined to do any research since I am not part of the bank staff or the IMF; but they did send a list of related agencies in Mexico that we may want to contact—out of courtesy, the note said. I thought that was pretty considerate of them. I also got some great reports from the Department of Commerce 'Flash Facts'. That was pretty amazing. I punched document numbers over the touch-tone phone along with my fax number—and, lo and behold, the reports I requested showed up in about 30 minutes. I was really impressed. It does seem that there are a lot of resources out there to access."

"Boy, that's no kidding." It was Joe who sounded enthusiastic now. "I received a fax from the American Chamber of Commerce, too. A one day turn-around, can you believe that! They sent about ten pages listing manufacturers and distributors of computer and data communications equipment. The list gives the company name and address, the products they make or sell, and the head person's name— or maybe the person who is the member of the Chamber. In any case, it identifies a person to call.

"I think they will be invaluable as a resource from which to get a list of companies that will be our prospective customers. I haven't called yet to ask for that. We have to decide on the industries and the criteria first. The people at the American Chamber are very helpful, but

I have to be able to narrow the search—short of everyone in Mexico who is a member company."

"You're right, Joe. I have found out a little more about customer requirements from some of the reports, but we still have to decide which industries we want to start with. Also, we need to consider some of the other potential screening criteria to narrow the customer list." Marlena was thinking of her past marketing experience and processes that had been used before to target specific customers. "Are we going to target medium sized companies or large? Shall we set a minimum annual revenue and growth rate that we will look for in a company? Of course, come to think of it, I am not certain that we can get things like annual reports or 10K reports on Mexican companies. They don't exactly have to publish for the New York Stock exchange or the SEC, do they? I wonder who conducts credit checks in Mexico, if anyone?"

"Another consideration we have to look at is the geography of the country." The team looked at Phil, a bit puzzled. "Well, do we want to concentrate on customers in Mexico City only? Do we want to sell product in Monterey, Guadalajara, Queretaro, or any other cities? Monterey and Guadalajara are both, more or less, on the inside of the two mountain ranges—although Guadalajara is starting to get up into the mountains a bit. I think we need to look at the impact the location has on shipping. I doubt that we will air ship all of our equipment, so where the customers are located will affect things like shipping costs, right?

"But wait till I tell you what else I discovered at the Department of Commerce regional office. There is a special service called a "Gold Key Service". When you sign up for Gold Key, the DOC post in the requested country—Mexico in our case—will provide an office, secretarial service, translator if needed, even a driver if you request. AND—most important, they will arrange four to six meetings a day for you with potential distributors, agents, or customers. They will even provide us with counseling on Mexican business practices while we are there."

"Are you kidding?" Bob was definitely skeptical. He had always believed the theory of 'no free lunch', and had seldom been proven wrong. "What's the catch? That must cost a fortune. You mean they actually screen companies and arrange meetings for us?"

"I am not kidding. Of course there is a charge, but I was amazed at how reasonable it is. The current rate is $350 for the first day, and $250 for each additional day. That covers an office and the arrangement of meetings. The secretarial and translator services are a little extra. They said a company usually takes 2-4 days; and you have to plan this six weeks in advance.

"This is only offered for products or services originating in the U.S.; but that is no problem for us since our plant for the GCB is in Bisbee and the AAB is made in Tempe. The foreign parts content is still less than 51%, isn't it?"

Joe jumped in at this point. "Oh yeah. When Bob and I assessed the features and functions for the Mexican market, we checked how many foreign components we use in the products. In the GCB, the exterior housing and the mylar pad are the only off-shore manufactured parts. If we decide to "harden" the product for Mexico, we will build a new housing, so only the pad will be foreign.

"So Phil, did you sign us up for the Gold Key?"

"Not yet. We will need to provide the DOC with information; and some of it we haven't decided yet. Among other things, we still have to determine what type of contacts we would want to make. Do we want to meet potential distributors?—Maybe joint venture partners—like that system integrator we were talking about. What sort of customers are we looking for?—you know, back to the criteria / screening questions. And, we have to send them pricing information. So we need to do a bit more strategizing before we can request that service."

"Well, I found out a little more about customer requirements." It was Marlena's turn, now. "For one thing, Mexican businessmen are really looking for vendor relationships that will cover the long-term. They don't exactly trust the U.S. quarter by quarter mentality. Those Mexican businesses that have been operating for a long time have been through a lot of ups and downs when you think of the Mexican economic history. It wasn't so long ago that inflation was over 100%, and the government controlled most everything. Now, they are seeing some economic turmoil again after almost of decade of getting things stabilized. This turmoil is expected to be temporary, but so many U.S. investors are backing off that both potential Mexican partners and customers are getting nervous about making their business dependent on U.S. companies and investors. They really are looking for vendors and partners who have a long term plan for business in Mexico, and are willing to weather the storms that are certain to occur.

"In addition to long term relationships, customers are also getting more sophisticated in negotiating for the extras. The Pyramid research report indicates that more current communications equipment sales have been clinched by the elements of the deal beyond the equipment itself. Things such as leasing terms, customer financing, after sale maintenance and service are now key differentiators. Of course, price is very important, too—as we talked about before. The competitors, especially the Asian companies, usually compete on price."

"It sounds as if the customer requirements there are similar to what we have learned here in the U.S. We need to consider the whole system to meet the customer needs. A lot of times, we have been able to offset the price of the equipment by saving cost in the overall network—consolidating physical links, improving reliability, simplifying network management—those kinds of things." Joe continued to relate some specific examples he remembered from the past year's win/loss reviews he had conducted. "In the cases where the Carlsbad Equipment distributor had considered the whole system -our products as well as other vendors' stuff in the network—they could show customers how the product meets multiple needs. I think that will be even more important in Mexico, from what I am learning. We can't expect the customer to have worked through the whole network design and recognize the benefits and savings to be gained when our equipment is put into their network."

Marlena added an important observation. "Besides, we have to keep in mind that many Mexican businesses are partnering with U.S. companies in their industry. They look to the U.S. partner to bring in the expertise needed to optimize technology; so in a lot of cases, the requirements and expectations for service will be the same as our customers here—actually, we can expect that some of the customer personnel really will be the same people.

"The technology requirements are already pretty sophisticated, though. Pyramid Research discussed the advanced services already being used by the large banks over their own networks. For instance, in some banks video conferencing is used to conduct meetings with sites outside Mexico City. Another example is Bancomer. They offer Point Of Sales service to over 15000 businesses in Mexico. You can imagine that their service and reliability requirements for that system is demanding. "

"Absolutely! And it is not only banks that have accelerated in technology. Bob Jr. came home from college over the weekend; and he was telling me all about the University in Monterey, Mexico. He said that they have real-time, interactive video classes for Physics. The classes are conducted across twenty remote campuses simultaneously so all of the University's students get the benefit of the Physics prof in Monterey. Actually, I had no idea that the Mexican universities had come that far, did you? I mean that really says the other universities are going to be a big market too."

"And there we are again, Bob." Marlena was again thinking of the critical criteria. "We know we can't enter a new market and be all things to all people—to use an old cliché. We are going to have to determine which industries to start with, and how to qualify specific customers."

"OK. I have a suggestion. Let's consider the criteria we already have, find lists of companies that meet those criteria so far, and then see what information is available to screen the companies down further."

"That's a good approach, Joe." Phil laughed, "I think I see some of that law department experience training on getting the specifics down in writing coming through. Here's the marker, why not put the ideas up on the white board."

"Well, we have said that we will probably first enter Mexico City, Guadalajara, and Monterey, so we need companies headquartered in those cities. We want companies in financial services for certain, and then we want to compare manufacturing opportunities against retail opportunities to see which is better for first entry."

As Marlena continued checking her notes, Bob added, "We also want to consider the Universities. If they have enough campuses as advanced as the University of Monterey, they would be a good first entry, too."

Marlena tentatively agreed, "I think you are right in the potential, Bob. But I am thinking that the Universities should be put into the same category as the government agencies for Carlsbad. We need to start making contacts in those segments, but usually the sales takes much longer, you have to respond to bids, and the biggest differentiator is price—the lowest bidder gets the job."

"Well, that's how it is in the U.S. We should check whether they operate the same way in Mexico. If the Universities are right on the verge of procuring data networks we wouldn't want to miss them, right?" Joe was speaking as he was writing the comments on the board. "So—now, just shout out sources of where we can get lists of companies that fit these requirements so far. I'll write it down, and then we can split up the sources and each pursue some and come back with our lists. OK—ready—I'll start with getting a list from the American Chamber of Commerce—"

"The Department of Commerce has an on-line search and retrieval system called the National Trade Data Bank (NTDB). It has all types of reports available on it. When I spoke with the person at the International Resource Center downtown, she said I should make an appointment and someone at the center will show me how to use it. You can search it for particular types of companies with a type of Boolean logic. For instance, you can select country = Mexico, companies = large, medium, or small, and product = steel. It sorts on all of those selections and comes up with a hit list. Then, you view the list and it gives you information about each company. She said it included things like the company's legal name, the address, telephone, and usually Fax number; when it was established; the product or service brief description; type of business the company is in—such as retail, wholesaler, distributor, etc.; and—very important—a contact person's name."

"That's great, Phil. Did you make an appointment yet?"

"Tomorrow at 10:00. They reserve the system for you for one hour."

"So—," Bob continued as if he had something more in mind. "When you get back from learning how to use the system, you and I can get together and sign on to it over the Internet, OK? I found a brochure for the Department of Commerce's 'Country Commercial Guides' that are available on the NTDB system and it gives the Internet address for accessing the data base. The commercial guides give information on market conditions; investment and financing; economic situation and the political environment; services available for exporters, trade regulations; AND, the best export sectors for that country. It sounds like something that will come in very handy."

"Great, let's keep going. Any other sources we should pursue?"

"We can call the Mexican Chamber of Commerce, and see if they publish a membership guide."

Marlena chuckled, "Well, that idea gives us good sources—but there is a whole hierarchy of Chambers of Commerce in Mexico. Businesses are mandated by the government to join the Chamber appropriate for their type of business. For instance, there is the Mexican Association of Stock Brokerage Firms; the Chamber of Commerce and Tourism for Small Businesses; the Businessmen's Coordinating

Council, and so on. One of my cousins works in a Chamber office in Hermosillo. She has explained the system to me before. It gets pretty complicated. The whole system is hierarchical and has its own reporting structure. Fortunately, when we are ready to register to do business in Mexico, the government will tell us exactly which Chamber we must join.

"Additionally, the states in Mexico have offices for the government mandated Chambers, so we need to contact the Monterey and Guadalajara offices, besides Mexico City for company information on potential customers and partners.

"Then, even further, there are voluntary associations for various industries. These associations are excellent sources of information on industry sectors, as well as opportunities for contacts through their membership. We would probably be interested in eventually joining CANIECE—Camara Nacional de la Industria Electronica y de Comunicaciones Electricas—or, in English, the National Chamber for the Electric and Electronic Communication Industries. Other specific associations can help us identify potential prospects—but they are quite specific as to type of product, such as apparel and textiles associations, chemicals associations, etc. We can use them to help screen the lists in the second round of criteria, I think.

"At this first go-round, however, I can call the city Chambers and get the city industrial directories. That should list a lot of the businesses in that city."

"Great, Marlena. Joe, how about also putting up there—'industry publications'. We can call *Communications Week, Information Week,* and some of the other key magazines and ask them to give us a list of the subscribers in Mexico. Those lists are usually pretty reasonable to purchase."

"Got it, Phil. What about the associations that Carlsbad Equipment already belongs to here in the U.S? What Marlena was saying made me think about our own memberships. Didn't the big industry association do a joint Mexico/ US show in Mexico last year—or host one in Houston for Mexican businesses, or something like that?"

"I think you're right, Joe. I'll give Stan a call over in communications and publicity and see if he can help us identify who we need to talk with.

"Well, let's get to it! Who is going to take which one to follow up? Let's get back together next Thursday, OK?"

On the next Thursday morning, the team was anxious to get started when Phil walked in. "Hi. Sorry I'm late. I had one of those impromptu hallway meetings—but this one was with Paul."

"Paul, as in Paul Esters, the CEO?"

"Yes, he is having a luncheon meeting with several members of the Board and wanted a brief update on our progress so far. He reconfirmed, and wanted me to be sure to pass on to you, that Carlsbad Equipment is absolutely serious about this venture into the Mexican market. I gently reiterated what you had said, Marlena, about the need to take a long term view and that we have to plan to stick it out with our Mexican customers and partners. He said he fully understands that, and there is no question that we are in this for the long haul. He would like for the whole team to attend the next Board of Directors meeting next month and discuss the opportunities in Mexico."

"OK! Well, I think we are going to have some interesting stuff to report."

Everyone laughed at Joe's comment. Bob asked, "Is that a marketing or legal term, Joe—'stuff'?"

"Ha—well, you know what I mean. Look at this." Joe handed everyone a copy of a Department of Commerce brochure. Reading the brochure headline, Joe quoted, "'We'll screen your foreign customers and prospective agents with our World Traders Data Reports.' Isn't this something?! The DOC does a qualifying report on any company we submit—buyers, distributors, or agents. A report takes about 45—90 days and provides all this information for only $100 per report." Reading again from the brochure, Joe continued,—"' Product lines; number of employees; capitalization of the company; bank and trade references; sales volume; reputation; key officers of managers.' They also try to include the company's subsidiaries and parent company if applicable. With what we understand of the Grupo concept in Mexico, I think that will be very helpful. The report lists the company's U.S. customers, branch locations, and recent news clips about the company—even activities of prominent owners of the company.

"Even if we requested 50 reports over a year, $5000 would be an insignificant investment compared to the cost of just one bad guess. I read about one company that assumed a distributor was solid because they were a big company so they put the distributor on open account. The manufacturer had over $125000 outstanding with that distributor when the distributor finally closed up in bankruptcy. This World

Traders Data Report service will save us a lot of risk and potential grief. As a matter of fact, the DOC said that the WTDR qualifies as one of the reports the Foreign Credit Insurance Association requires before giving coverage to the exporter."

Marlena was thinking out loud as she commented, "I wonder if the embassy DOC people can really respond that quickly. After all, how many people make requests?"

"I wondered that too; but while I was gathering brochures I spoke with a gentleman from Tempe who had used this service. He said that for a little while, during the 'boom' period, the DOC staff was overworked and had too many requests. Now, however, they have really prioritized helping get U.S. companies started into Mexico; and, of course, things have slowed down a little. He indicated the response was really good now and the people are intent on being helpful." Joe concluded, "This fellow said some of the DOC staff are a little naive about real everyday business, but they are bright and helpful people who can assist a company starting up."

"That sounds pretty good. I discovered a source to help check out companies in Mexico, too. It isn't nearly as formal, and we would have to qualify the qualifiers—so this is just a last check point, so to speak." Everyone looked at Bob, puzzled. He continued, "As we were going through information on the Internet, I saw a reference to Mexnet, a private conference-bulletin board type service out of Utah. I signed on to check it out. Mexnet is a service subscribed to by both U.S. and Mexican companies to share information and conversation, really. When you sign on, you identify if you will converse in Spanish or English. The fee is nominal and based on usage, so I signed up. I figure it can be a great source where we can launch a question about a company, a policy, a custom, or whatever and get a variety of perspectives and responses back. At least it is worth testing out, right?"

"Absolutely! Sometimes personal leads gained over a service like that are priceless." Marlena added her findings, too. "I ran across an ad for reports specifically pertaining to the manufacturing sector. The Economist Intelligence Unit of the Economist magazine group publishes Industrial Development Reviews they develop with the United Nations Industrial Development Organization. It is a high level review of the Mexican industrial framework, government economic policy, macroeconomic trends AND—prospects for each industrial sector. The report costs $150, so—now I have spent a little of our money. I ordered it yesterday."

"Great." Now it was Phil who was particularly anxious to get down to work. "Let's start combining all of these lists everyone brought from the various sources; see which ones overlap; see which sectors look the most promising with number of prospects, etc. ; and then figure out which contact we want to use to qualify which companies."

After a couple weeks work the team had requested three specific reports from the DOC. One had been on file which the team received right away. The other two were being researched. They decided that it was time Phil and Joe traveled to Mexico to begin to get a flavor of the market and, hopefully, begin to make a few contacts. They still hadn't gathered all the information, or made all the decisions needed to apply for the Gold Key Service, but expected that to be a third quarter event.

Marlena stopped by Phil's office. "Are you and Joe getting excited about your first official trip to Mexico City?"

"Boy, that's for sure. There is so much to do. I've been trying to pick prospective customers out of our list that are close together so I can get from one to another quickly, so I'm trying to map their addresses on this street map. I figure we can get to three in the morning and three in the afternoon. Two days of that and we should gather some good first hand information about the customer requirements, who they use as distributors, how they buy data equipment, where—"

"Whoa, Phil. What are you talking about? That's way too many appointments for a day in Mexico City—especially since these people don't know you."

"What do you mean. I figure, especially *because* they don't know us we will be lucky to get half an hour with each. You know how hard it is to get executives' time—even in our own existing customers."

"That's here, Phil,—in the U.S. Mexican business is conducted differently. Slow down a bit. First, you will be much better off if a mutual acquaintance calls the prospect beforehand and introduces you. Then, when you call for an appointment, the Mexican executive will be anticipating your call and will know who you are. Remember? That's why we checked which of our current customers are already doing business in Mexico. They can make some of the contacts for you. Maybe the American Chamber of Commerce can help, too.

"Then, once you have an appointment, you must plan to spend considerable time—maybe two or more hours—with the executive. It must be his schedule you accommodate—not yours. If you book back to back appointments, and one of the Mexican people is talking with you, you would either have to excuse yourself and leave, or be late for your other appointment. Either way, that is inexcusable rudeness in Mexico. They will never abruptly terminate a conversation with someone just to meet an appointment. The person they are speaking with is considered important."

"But, Marlena!" Now it is Phil who interrupts. "I already made some of the appointments and talked with the secretaries. I told them what time my earlier appointment is and where I would be coming from. None of them even suggested that keeping the appointments would be difficult. They all immediately put me down on their boss's calendar."

"Of course, Phil. In Mexico, it is not the secretary's place to second guess either their boss or you. They will put it down on the calendar assuming you know what you want to do. Their boss may or may not even be planning to be there; but if you request that specific time, they will write it down assuming you and the boss will work it out. Chances are, when you arrive you may find out he is in a meeting or at lunch. Did you remember that a lot of business is conducted over the lunch meal which begins around 2:00 PM and can go till 4:00 or 4:30?"

Phil looked a little sheepish. "I guess my appointments at 3:00 and 4:00 probably aren't too solid, huh?"

"Why don't I help you plan your schedule, OK? Also, Phil," Marlena hesitated not wanting to chide Phil too much, but recognized he desperately needed some coaching. "You really are expecting to gain too much at your first encounter with these people. In Mexico, the business people will not immediately tell you all about their business requirements, or how they buy equipment—and they certainly will not tell you about their current distributor before they know you. Relationships are very important—among business people as well as among friends. They have a relationship with their distributor, and even if service isn't the greatest, they wouldn't tell a complete stranger that—especially, someone from the U.S. They have to have time to get to know *you*—not just Carlsbad Equipment, but you—Phil Sierra. In Mexico the old adage is really true—people do business with people."

"Well, that's true here too, Marlena. American businessmen prefer to conduct business with people they like. But they can keep business separate from personal relationships most of the time. Business is business."

"Phil, here in the U.S. we have an established and perhaps, overused, judicial system. A businessman doesn't have to know you personally to conduct business. He signs a contract with Carlsbad Equipment and expects the company to stand behind it. If it fails, he has the option to sue the company and get his money back, often plus an additional amount for the effort.

"It isn't the same in Mexico. The court system is neither so prolific nor efficient nor—in some cases—quite so up-front. A Mexican businessman needs to be able to trust the person he is doing business with. He has to feel comfortable that you are honest and forthright, and both willing and able to protect his interest in your company. Recourse is not so easy as it is in the U.S. This is slowly changing in parts of Mexico, but history has created a cultural aspect to business that says you have to spend time to get to know one another before you launch into a big discussion of how the Mexican businessman does business."

"So what am I supposed to talk about in the first meeting?"

"Be sociable, Phil. Talk a little about Carlsbad Equipment, its history, and its plans; but spend more time talking about you. And, more important, allow him to spend time talking about Mexico and about himself. That doesn't mean he will share all of his personal history, or problems, or anything—Mexicans are very private people—, but he will begin to provide you some information that will give you insight into his own character and beliefs. Most important—don't rush.

"It would be really great if you could find out some history beforehand. If you have a mutual contact that can tell you what the person's hometown is and how he has progressed through the company, then you can do a little research on that town and have something to ask him about. I'll help you with the background and history of places in Mexico. The Mexican prospect will greatly appreciate your taking the time and having the interest to have found out a little about the country and especially his home."

"Thanks, Marlena. I guess I got a little too caught up in the excitement and potential for all this business, ha ha. Any other hints I should hear. I really am listening."

"Well, since you asked—while you are there, one of your appointments might be with CANIECE. Remember—the National Chamber for the Electric and Electronic Communication Industries? If you can begin to make some contacts there and soon, attend some of their meetings, it will pay off enormously later on in contacts, help with trade events, etc. The more Carlsbad Equipment gets involved in associations and business events, the better it will be known and appreciated."

"Got it."

A couple weeks later, Phil and Joe checked into the hotel in Mexico City. They were staying near Chapultepec Park in the center of the city. The concierge spoke perfect English, and Joe was asking him about art museums in the city. "There is, of course, the Palace of Fine Art that you should see. In the park, there is Tamayo's museum as well that—"

Phil stepped beside Joe and inquired as to what they were discussing.

"I was asking about art museums we might see while we are here. I always believe that viewing some of the classic art of a country helps you get a feeling for the history and culture."

The concierge continued, "This is true—and so you must take time to walk in the city and view the murals, one of Mexico's significant contributions to the world of modern art."

"Murals?" Phil was curious. "You mean on walls, sort of like graffiti?"

"Not exactly, sir. In the 1920's and '30's, after the revolution, some of the country's most famous artists were also political activists. Diego Rivera, in particular, began a muralist movement and was able to get commissioned to paint great works on the modern buildings of the time. Rivera believed that art should be for the masses, so it should be seen in places where all the people can enjoy it. His work is very emotional and usually shows the struggle of the peasants and the political environment of Mexico. Orozco and Siqueiros followed suite and also painted great murals. Tamayo preferred to preserve the classic media of canvas and often debated the need to maintain traditional art. They were a very colorful group in the art society in those days."

"Thank you. Can you give us the hours the museums are open, please? I would really like to see some of this work." Joe was anticipating some free time, the next morning.

The next day at the office of the CANIECE, Phil met Sr. Enrique Garcia Fuentes. Sr. Garcia Fuentes was a computer science specialist who had done his undergraduate work in London, England and received his Masters of Science at MIT. As a matter of fact, most of the people Phil had met this morning had studied abroad or in the U.S., and were extremely polished.

Phil was sincerely impressed by the knowledge of this man, Sr. Garcia Fuentes, as well as with his broad experiences. He had traveled extensively in Europe and the United States, and was comparing some of the great cities of the world to Mexico City for Phil.

"By the way, Sr. Sierra. Have you met Sr. Paco Guererra Montemayor?" Sr. Garcia Fuentes had a curious twinkle in his eye.

"No sir. I haven't had the pleasure."

"Sr. Guererra is a very respected businessman here in Mexico City; and is very active on the Board of Directors of CANIECE. He has a personal interest in expanding Mexico's technological base and views U.S. companies interested in Mexico as a very positive influence for Mexico's growth. He has a home in Tucson, Arizona, and has taken an interest in companies in that state in the U.S."

With a little more conversation, Sr. Garcia Fuentes politely indicated to Phil that some U.S. companies seem to have better success getting started in Mexico when they have a Mexican businessman on their Board of Directors; particularly, if the Mexican is well connected with business in Mexico and takes an active interest in coaching the American company. Phil listened attentively and resolved to speak to Paul Esters as soon as possible. Sr. Garcia Fuentes indicated he was calling Sr. Guererra this week regarding some current issues, and would mention his conversation with Phil.

The Carlsbad Equipment Corp. Board of Directors' meeting was in three weeks. Phil was excited about the prospect of inviting Sr. Guererra to attend and meet the people. Another action item to do!

CHAPTER 7

The Intermediaries

The team was really excited after the Board of Directors' meeting. The presentation had gone very well; and although they couldn't answer all of the questions yet, the Board was not backing off their commitment to conducting business in Mexico.

Paul Esters seemed to truly enjoy the company of Sr. Guererra and was careful to personally introduce him to every member of the Board. Over the past few weeks, Phil and Paul had met with Sr. Guererra several times — primarily over dinner that tended to last 2 3 hours. Phil had reminded himself that he would have to get used to that custom since Marlena kept telling him it was the way people get to know each other in Mexico.

Paco Guererra Montemayor was just as Sr. Garcia Fuentes described him. He was a pleasant, jovial sort of man who also happened to be extremely bright. Educated in Germany, Spain, and the U.S., Sr. Guererra had been very successful in the Mexican construction business. He also had expanded the business into Chile and Argentina, and was beginning to talk with the Chinese. As Sr. Garcia Fuentes had said, Sr. Guererra was passionate about the need for advanced data communications in Mexico. He whole heartedly believed that technology and especially communications technology would be key to Mexico's future growth. His brother, the mayor of Guadalajara, deeply agreed with him; and often asked Paco to assist with the mayor's presentations at meetings with the Secretary of Communications and Transportation. In the new Mexican government administration, local officials have more autonomy than before and tend to interpret regulations to benefit their constituency. It would be very helpful if, through his brother's experience, Sr. Paco Guererra had knowledge of where to find answers about regional laws and regulations in addition to his business knowledge. Phil was confident that Sr. Guererra would accept the planned invitation to be a member of the Carlsbad Equipment Board, and was very pleased with the idea of the advice that Sr. Guererra would be able to provide.

Actually, the soon-to-be Board member was already offering advice. Based on his polite hints, the Board of Directors had given the team some fairly specific directives.

"So, if I was listening well, I think we just got the go-ahead to start talking with that systems integrator about a joint marketing partnership, right?" Bob was ready to pick up the pace of the team's efforts.

"Well, they were definitely interested in our suggestion." Phil knew Bob well enough to recognize that he would soon have to channel Bob's energies. "I think Sr. Guererra is going to help us with that one. At the coffee break, he told Paul that he would check into that company a little. With the economy being in such turmoil right now, it is important to find out about a company's structure. You know—who really owns them; how is their debt structured—are they stretched out in dollar denominated debt; who are the major customers, and how solid are they; are accounts receivable collectable—those sort of things that would be hard to find out in a casual conversation. They might never tell you and me, but Sr. Guererra will be able to talk with them very directly.

"The Board also wants us to check out some other distributors; and, this time, I have an idea of just where to start."

Joe started laughing. "Why do I get the feeling we are heading back downtown to the Department of Commerce?"

"Exactamente—my friend! The DOC offers an Agent/Distributor Service. The trade specialists here will help us prepare the information and sales literature, and then they will send it to the commercial specialists in Mexico. Those people contact potential distributors and evaluate their interest and capabilities. They will give us a list of up to six of the top qualified candidates with the name, address, and phone for contacting them. The ADS people even assess the candidate's capability and current activities in their report." Phil was excited now.

"What types of factors do they assess, Phil?" Bob had followed Phil into his office.

"Well, according to this 'Basic Guide to Exporting' from the DOC, they have a pretty inclusive check-list. Look at this, Bob."

As Bob read the list out loud, he became more comfortable that the ADS people would indeed know what to look for, "Size of sales force, sales record, objectives and long-range expansion plans, territorial analysis, plans for new branch offices, product mix, companies currently represented, facilities and equipment inventory such as warehousing space and computer facilities, marketing policies, customer profiles and what percentage of revenue are from top customers, promotional policies and budget—Wow! I guess this would be a pretty comprehensive report, wouldn't it?

"So, we are getting together tomorrow morning, right? I'd like the team to review our current criteria for distributor selection and see if we need to consider anything different—or maybe just weight the criteria differently—or something. I think we will have to give these ADS people a pretty clear picture of what we can and can't provide to a distributor, and what sort of qualifiers Carlsbad Equipment would typically use."

"You are absolutely right, Bob. The DOC people can't do their job without our very specific input. I'm sure they will want to work with us very closely. We will also be doing our own research too. The ultimate choice of distributor or distributors should be the best we can select from all the available sources. And, I am really happy that we will have Mr.—I mean—Sr. Guererra's help in the final decision and selection.

"Hey—I'll see you in the morning. I have to take my son John to the tux shop before they close. Can you feature it—at the ripe old age of 14 he is going to be in his cousin's wedding. Ha, Sarah is already an old pro at weddings. Ten years old and she has been in four so far. But John is a bit nervous so I promised Mary that I would take him to get his fitting. See you tomorrow."

The next morning the team was discussing the various methods Carlsbad Equipment had used in the past to select distributors. Marlena was speaking, "There is a big difference to keep in mind, however. In the U.S., Carlsbad has always had to seriously court a distributor and sometimes offer pretty sweet deals to get them to begin carrying our product—until they find out it is well accepted in their market. In Mexico, it is Carlsbad who will get courted; and just like a young debutante, we will need to be careful not to let the flattery sway our decisions."

"Just what do you mean, Marlena?" Joe had expected that it would be difficult to find distributors in Mexico.

"Mexico is a rather new market economy. There are a lot a people trying to start their businesses, and a lot of them are hoping to capitalize on the demand for data technologies. The distributors are looking for U.S. technology to build their companies around. Carrying U.S. products helps them gain credibility quickly. That is not a bad thing, if they can support it. However, sometimes they get the cart in front of the horse, so to speak. They want to sign up a U.S. supplier before they have the capital, or trained employees, or support structure to implement their plans. My cousin tells me that a lot of U.S. companies have come to Mexico and gotten so caught up in the enthusiasm of so many distributors trying to gain their attention and their business, that they jump in too quickly. The U.S. companies forget that you can't take anything for granted. It is very important to really know the distributors you select. The truly credible ones want much more than just the ability to advertise U.S. product. They want a manufacturer / supplier who is interested in helping them be successful and grow their business. In return, they will be very anxious to meet the requirements the manufacturer."

"I have an idea. When we have selected the top five or so, why don't we invite each one of them here to Phoenix." Bob was still thinking of how to accelerate the processes. "They could meet our whole team at once; and we could show them the Carlsbad Equipment operations. Between all of us, we could give them the royal treatment, show them around, and be checking them out all at the same time."

"I don't think that will work so well, Bob." Joe was considering Bob's suggestion. "From what I have been able to learn so far, I get the feeling that the trip here to Carlsbad Equipment should be further down the line of conversations and meetings. The Mexican businessmen won't want us to show off how great the operation is here, and how wonderful everything is in the U.S. I'm afraid that we will come across as the demanding, 'all-knowing', '*ugly*' American if we force them to come to us right at first with a formal invitation. They will want to see our operations in due time. However,—correct me if I'm wrong—I think they will be much more impressed if Phil and one or two others of the team went to them. They want to see that we take an interest in seeing *their* operations. Give them a chance to show off how they do things. Besides, being there would give them and us more time to relax and be sociable where they are comfortable—on their own 'turf'."

"I would tend to agree with your assessment, Joe." Phil was rather impressed by Joe's increasing sensitivity to the cultural questions. "What if we arranged the meetings there; and asked Paul Esters to go with us. If the CEO of Carlsbad Equipment comes to see their operation, they would certainly believe that CE is serious about starting business in Mexico, and that we are interested in their success."

"Great! How soon do you think he would be available to go?" Bob was still hoping for speed.

"Umm—Wait a sec." Marlena was obviously uncomfortable with Phil's idea. "Having the CEO visit the operations and attend the meetings would certainly indicate our level of interest, but it could cause us some big problems later on."

"How so, Marlena?"

"There are two concerns. First, we might embarrass our potential new partner if they cannot match levels. If CE's CEO attends, they will have to have the person there who is the equivalent level in their company. Mexican business is extremely 'level conscious'—peers talk to peers, and decisions are deferred to the top boss. That is the second issue. Once they begin dealing with Paul Esters, they will automatically assume that all decisions are to be made by him. Phil and the rest of us will not be able to reach any conclusions.

"My suggestion is to have the meetings in Mexico as Joe stated, but to keep it at Phil's level from Carlsbad Equipment. You have to be perceived as the person with the authority to make the deal, Phil. 'Empowerment' just isn't something that has happened in Mexico, yet. Everything takes extra time because everything goes through the channels, and each level waits for the next to make a decision and pass it up to the next level. If you are seen as the 'boss in charge' you will be able to deal with people at the top level in the Mexican organization. If Paul Esters is there, he will have to be the one to finalize all the decisions from then on."

"That's good to know, Marlena." Phil was trying to think through a likely transaction. "I suppose we will have to be sure to talk with top level in the distributor's organization, right?"

"Oh, absolutely. My aunt in Hermosillo told me about a U.S. company working with the shoe manufacturer where she works. The U.S. negotiators went through all the steps to get a contract signed, but never reached the top level. Someone lower in the Mexican company signed the contract, and the top boss was more angry at the U.S. team than at his own people. I guess the Mexican company is going to honor the contract, but it will take a lot of apologizing from the U.S. company to mend the relationship."

Bob was confounded. "I don't get it. Why wouldn't the top guy be furious with his own people if they signed a contract?"

Marlena had to smile as she thought about the question. "I suppose because he knows that everyone 'wants their picture with the fish.'"

"What?"

"Remember when we discussed that people take business very personally and so no one wants to be associated with a problem. Just so, everyone wants to be perceived as 'in charge', and be associated with the successes. The phrase comes from the coastal towns; if someone catches a prize fish, everyone on the boat wants to have their picture taken with the fish so they can feel they had part in the success. If the U.S. people were willing to give the authority to a lower level by having that person sign the contract, that person would probably be too embarrassed to tell the U.S. team they were mistaken. Keep in mind, the 'people relationship' is more important than the 'business relationship', and no one will directly tell you 'no'. Besides, I'm sure the person signing wanted to be seen as the boss.

"It is very important to gain a 'coach' inside the Mexican company—distributor or customer—so you know who to deal with, as well as how well you are progressing. Otherwise, you may think you are on the right track and about to win the contract, when come to find out, you are not even in consideration. The Mexican businessman doesn't want to bring bad news, or humiliate the other party."

"This is getting confusing. For now, why don't we talk a little about our criteria for selecting distributors." Bob was getting a bit perplexed. "We can use that check-list Phil has from the DOC ADS program and set some parameters for the various aspects."

The team continued the discussion and established a range of parameters for such elements such as size of sales force, revenues, and promotional budget. They were more specific on such things as desired customer profile by industry and size, other products represented—so they would have complimentary families of products—and especially geographic coverage.

When the group reached the question regarding computer facilities, Joe spoke up. He had obviously given the subject some thought. "I think the distributors we select should be fairly well versed in computer technology; and preferably, already have access to a data communications network. For one thing, that would certainly add to their credibility for selling data communications equipment. If they use it themselves, they will know what the customers face.

"But maybe more important, if they are familiar with the tools, we can hopefully utilize some of the advanced marketing information systems we have installed with our U.S. distributors over the past year and a half."

Bob was curious. "I've heard a little about this system, but I haven't actually seen it demonstrated. What does it do, Joe?"

"We have built an electronic data base that we can share with our distributors. Each one, of course, only has access to their own customers from the centralized file. But, take our proposed system integrator, joint-marketing partner, for instance. The marketing tool could be shared between them and CE. It would identify cross-border customers that both parties are supporting and show what they have as the installed base in the various locations, what equipment is on order for delivery to where by when, and what is the potential for system integration.

"Besides identifying potential new business, the cross-border systems integration teams could use the system to communicate about the progress of the system in that account. For instance, we could set up a 'groupware conference system' that everyone on the account could use for communication among each other."

"How is that any different than our E-Mail system now, Joe?" Now, Phil was curious too.

"The conference is similar to an Internet bulletin board, only just accessible by authorized users. Everyone working on the account could be allowed to access the conference. This way, anyone dealing with that customer could sign on at any time and immediately get up to speed on the latest events—who called on whom, any open issues, what had been resolved and how, etc. The conference keeps everyone's correspondence filed according to subject so the account team can always be immediately up to date—no matter where they are located.

"Since Marlena's research indicated that customer service is becoming more important, we can also include the customer service data base. That one gives a specific escalation path defined by the customer, the distributor, and CE in case of unresolved issues. Everyone on the team can be aware of any product or service issues and the current status.

"Then—" Joe was excited as he thought about future prospects. "As soon as we finalize the electronic configurator, we will roll that out to the distributors as well. No reason not to include the Mexican distributors if they are on a network. The configurator verifies the equipment and prints out a quotation. Once the sale is made, the order is automatically loaded on the factory via standard EDI—but this system also orders documentation and identifies pertinent training the salesperson may want to recommend."

Phil was a little cautious. "It sounds almost too good to be true. We have to be a little careful on what we promise the people in the Mexican distributors. Here, we are used to hearing about systems like this for a year in advance, knowing that they are still in development and have to be tested out. From what I understand, the people in Mexico take your word and expect you to deliver right away. We have to watch what we say. A system like that might not be implementable for each distributor, depending on their location, the availability of a network, and their unique talents and level of sophistication with computers.

"Don't get me wrong. The system would be terrific. I just want everyone to be careful not to set expectations for our potential partners that we can't deliver."

Marlena had been listening carefully. "You are absolutely right, Phil. I've even read of cases in the Mexican courts in which the judge upheld the customer's complaint because the seller had verbally stated something and not delivered. Word of intent is taken at full value by Mexican businessmen.

"But, wow! Think of the marketing information we would have with that system. Our team could analyze that data base and find out what elements of our marketing strategy were working and which needed changing. We could check which industries are buying; what are they buying; are the products meeting customer needs as is or are special configurations showing up frequently—and if so, what special configurations can be standardized as product enhancements. We could—"

"Whoa." Now it was Bob who was laughing at Marlena's enthusiasm. "I can see this idea is going to take some strategizing itself. We are out of time today. Let's pick this one up first thing in the morning."

"And we have to keep in mind," Phil smiled as everyone headed out the door, "Marlena keeps reminding us that in Mexico, people buy from people. The marketing information system will be great as a tool to help check and constantly enhance our strategies; but you have convinced me that face to face relationships are what will really keep us ahead."

The next week, the team was reviewing their list of criteria regarding distributors with Sr. Guererra. "Please keep in mind as you are planning your negotiations with potential companies, Mr. Sierra, distributors in Mexico typically do not maintain an inventory of parts for service. When you put yourself in their shoes you can understand this. Over the past few years, our inflation rates have gone from well over 100% per year to 9% and now are near 60%. Hopefully, this is a temporary situation. However, if you were a distributor in Mexico, a high priced inventory of parts that was financed in U.S. dollars with a U.S. manufacturer could quickly create financial havoc for the Mexican distributor. No?

"Also, traditionally my people are very good at being reactive. We are used to fixing things when they break; so a distributor will get the part when it is needed rather than guess which parts to stock in advance."

"I can see your point, Sr. Guererra. Marlena has been helping us understand some of the differences in a distributor's business in Mexico as compared to the U.S. Her aunt works at a shoe manufacturer in Hermosillo, but we have been learning how to apply some of her experiences to our own situation. She has told us that it is difficult for a distributor to sell a maintenance contract to her company; and she also mentioned that the people are used to reacting to fix something. She said proactive avoidance is a different idea for people to consider. Additionally, Marlena's aunt pointed out that people don't want to pay for something in advance; and of course, a maintenance contract is much like an insurance policy—paid for before it is really needed. I guess they perceive it as a supplier using their money, so to speak; and I understand they resent that."

"Good, good! Then I imagine that you will plan for Carlsbad Equipment to provide a service center with stocking parts, etc. in Mexico, correct?"

Joe spoke up next. "We have been discussing the need to establish an office for Carlsbad in Mexico, even with a distributor arrangement. Marlena's research and the Department of Commerce reports indicate that our competitors already have offices there. We have pretty well decided that CE will need one for distributor support, customer and distributor training, promotional coordination with joint marketing partners, and partly just to have a presence there so people know the brand name, right?"

Sr. Guererra was smiling broadly, and added with a wink, "And you will find an office directly linked with CE here to be an added benefit in many ways. For instance, I might suggest that you consider your own electronic delivery to your own office for such things as documentation, order acknowledgments, and -very important— customer bills."

Joe was surprised. "Customer bills? But Sr., CE always mails our bills the same day that the shipping documents are printed. It is all part of our EDI electronic system. That system has improved our average receivable by 8—15 days!"

"Yes, I understand that, Mr. Tricot. Mr. Esters showed me your wonderful system. It is something to be very proud of. But you must consider that in Mexico we do not have such a sophisticated and reliable mail system as here in the United States. Things that must be delivered are usually personally delivered by hand. Now, of course, as the networks are becoming more extensive and reliable, electronic delivery is often used when possible. But the mail—tsk,tsk,—not something to rely on."

"Thank you, Sr. Now I understand your point." Joe felt a bit sheepish for having been so boastful about the CE system, and simply assuming that Sr. Guererra just didn't understand its benefits.

"Sr. Guererra," Phil broke what seemed to Joe to be an interminable silence, although it was actually only a second or so, "We have been discussing where would be the best place for Carlsbad's office. I understand the government will offer some tax incentives and benefits to companies that are willing to locate outside of Mexico City. I can easily see why the government would want to have companies spread around a little—to provide employment in other parts of the country and to help alleviate the tremendous population pressure on Mexico City. Since you are very familiar with both Mexico City and Guadalajara, I was hoping you might give us your opinion on location."

"It is true that the Mexican government does try to entice companies to move into areas other than Mexico City. Also, cities such as Guadalajara actively solicit companies to move into their areas as well, just as cities do here in the U.S. Ha, I have noticed Phoenix has competed recently with Houston, Texas to entice the large retailer from the East to move its headquarters into Phoenix.

"Nevertheless, the government is mostly interested in having manufacturing plants spread into different parts of the country. The office for Carlsbad Equipment is not manufacturing, and will not employ so many as a manufacturing plant. The majority of your customers are most likely to be headquartered in Mexico City; and the infrastructure you will need in the way of transportation, communications, and trained employees are all to be found in Mexico City. So, for your office to best support your distributors, I suspect you will find Mexico City the most suitable place.

"I will be in Mexico City for business in three weeks. Perhaps it would be convenient for you to plan your next trip to be at that time. It would be a pleasure for me to show you some of the sights of the city, and we can see some of the various commercial areas you might consider for an office."

"Thank you very much for the invitation Sr. Guererra. We will be there to meet with you at your convenience." Phil was genuinely thrilled with the prospect of having this very personable gentleman show them the fine points of the city.

Phil had convinced Paul Esters that the entire team needed to make the trip to Mexico this time. He explained that it was important that everyone gain a first hand experience of business in Mexico, that it was important to maintain a team spirit and sense of commitment, and that each person would notice things from a different perspective and thus make the trip much more valuable for the overall project. Paul finally agreed that the cost was nominal compared to the expected investment and ultimate payback in the long run for getting the right start when Carlsbad Equipment entered the Mexican market.

Paco Guererra Montemayor had arranged a meeting between the Carlsbad Equipment team and a well established distributor who could act almost as a consultant to answer some of the team's many questions. Sr. Luis Xavier Gayol, the country manager for the distributor's Mexican operation was a very hospitable and intelligent gentleman.

Phil noted that Sr. Xavier was approximately the same age as Phil—which seemed almost ancient here in Mexico City. Although just nearing 41, Phil had commented to Sr. Guererra that he felt as if he were a senior citizen in Mexico. Laughing, Paco had agreed with Phil, much to his chagrin, and then explained that 60% of Mexico's population was under the age of 25. "It is a very youthful, exuberant place—hopeful and energetic in the hearts of the young."

Sr. Luis Xavier had earned his undergraduate degree in engineering science at the University of Mexico and then went on to Paris to study for his masters in business. He spoke fluent Spanish, of course, but also French and Portuguese as well as English. He had worked as a consultant in Arthur D. Little before accepting the position he now held with this international distributor.

"As you suggest, Mr. Tricot, it is imperative that Carlsbad Equipment retain an attorney who is very familiar with the laws and regulations in Mexico to work with your corporate counsel. Also, of course, the NAFTA can be very confusing unless you have legal counsel familiar with international trade and tariff who has studied the agreement and understands its ramifications." Sr. Xavier had been describing his experiences at the time he opened the Mexican office for his company. "An important point to remember, which most international law attorneys know yet once in awhile forget, is to always include an arbitration clause in any contract with a Mexican business— your distributor or your customer. No one plans to have unreconcilable issues, but in case they should happen, you should be certain to designate how and where such issues will be arbitrated."

The next question was Phil's. "Sr. Xavier, do you believe it will be possible to find a distributor/ partner who is dedicated to customer service. 24 hour a day, 7 days a week service has always been a trademark for Carlsbad Equipment Corp. Our U.S. customers know they can always count on us to get their network up and running, even when the base fault is not our equipment. Our service techs stay on site until the problem is diagnosed and fixed no matter what or who caused it. I get the impression that customer service and that sense of urgency is not a common concept here in Mexico. People seem to react to fix things, but not until the problem has turned into a crisis and everything has crashed."

"Ah, Mr. Sierra, it seems that your question is really several. Yes I do believe you will find distributors here who are dedicated to customer service. As more data communications equipment suppliers enter our market, competitive differentiators are becoming more sophisticated. Certainly customer service is one of the differentiators. Also, as more companies learn to become efficient and competitive themselves, and start to depend on data networks for their business, customer service becomes more important to the customer. And—customer expectations are rising as well. Mexican businessmen expect U.S. technology to perform as well as they have heard or read; or their U.S. partners have educated them to expect performance, reliability, and service.

"What you will find here are people eager to learn technology and proud to do an excellent job. Our infrastructure and our economics have not provided too many people with the opportunity to have become proficient at servicing data communications equipment. However, if CE is able to provide training, you will discover the people are happy to learn and appreciative of the education. Many technicians in my company, after working around the clock to complete an installation on time, will take pictures of their work and show them to me with great pride."

Joe had been listening intently. "We were discussing that apparent eagerness to please and the sense of pride about doing an excellent job at dinner last evening. Phil and I met with a potential distributor yesterday afternoon, and just at the end of the very cordial meeting, the president of the company surprised us with his request. He invited us to return to spend more time with him and the people, and especially, to describe in detail exactly how Carlsbad Equipment would like salesmen to represent our products and how orders should be processed for CE. He indicated that before we even agreed that they would be a distributor, he wanted us to do a complete walk through of our processes with the administrative and sales people to ensure the CE process is done correctly. I cannot remember the last time a U.S. distributor was that eager to learn our systems or to please us. Usually, we have to bend to meet their systems."

Phil was also reviewing last evening's conversation in his mind. "Sr. Xavier, another point we were discussing was the topic of 'incentives.' I had assumed that distributors and salespeople here are incented that same as they are in the U.S., and I think everywhere—with dollar bonuses and recognition, right? I mean, Carlsbad Equipment Corp. has always had a great bonus program. When a distributor reaches 150% of the contracted quota, the distributor and the top salespeople begin getting some serious cash benefits. Then, once a year, the top distributor wins a very nice vacation trip. The incentive program works well for the distributor, the salespeople, and CE as well because we have always used it to promote new products or services to get them off to a fast start. Joe seemed to be concerned that things might be different here."

Politely smiling, Sr. Xavier thought about the question a moment. "Mr. Tricot has perhaps noticed a key difference between the cultures of Mexico and the U.S. Individualism is very important in the U.S. People feel that they individually do an excellent job for which they are very proud, and they appreciate being recognized and rewarded for that effort. Thus, in the U.S., people enjoy competing for the awards you described.

"In Mexico, it is a little different. In the U.S., a distributorship is a company; here, it is more of a family. The distributor will appreciate incentives that provide more training, or equate to cooperative advertising dollars he can spend, etc. He will look for things that will help advance his business. Additionally, the distributor and the salespeople appreciate family oriented incentives—perhaps CE could sponsor a family picnic, or salespeople may win points that add up to scholarships for their children. Being singled out among the peers that one works with on a daily basis is not always a good thing here. Although each individual personality is certainly unique, the company is more of a community than I have noticed in the U.S."

"So, Joe, you are right. We will have to spend some time re-thinking the incentive program for CE's Mexican distributors. "Phil noticed his watch—2:30 p.m. "Perhaps you would join us for lunch, Sr. Xavier? We would sincerely appreciate more of your insight on this topic, as well as many others. I believe our questions will last as long as the time you can allow us."

As the group was walking toward the restaurant, Joe paused. "Speaking of more questions—I have been wondering what those guys are doing with the portable typing machines, sitting out there on the benches, typing away? They certainly seem very busy."

Bob almost leaped forward to catch up to Joe. "This one I can answer. I asked about that yesterday. Those guys are notary publics. Practically every transaction here has to be notarized, and there is a hierarchy of notaries. These fellows are sort of the lower level who can notarize an everyday type of transaction. For instance, some banks still require that you have a withdrawal slip notarized before they will release your money. So, you can walk outside, find one who isn't busy, and he will notarize your transaction—complete with carbon copies. They higher level notaries serve as what we would consider a paralegal.

They have offices, and notarize the documents for major transactions. They play quite an important role in Mexican business. Interesting, huh?"

"I'm really impressed, Bob." Joe was laughing at Bob's enthusiasm in sharing his newly acquired knowledge.

After lunch, Sr. Xavier departed for his office and Paco Guererra escorted the team back to their hotel before taking his leave. Once alone again, in the lobby, Phil stopped the group before they headed for their rooms. "OK. What's going on here? Joe, why is it that you suddenly started referring to me as Mr. Sierra? I felt like I had just aged 25 years. And, Marlena, I don't think I heard you say two sentences all day! I'd like to know what's happening?."

Joe was the first to speak. "I really wasn't trying to be a smart aleck, Phil. I couldn't help notice how very formal Sr. Xavier and Sr. Guererra treated each other and all of us. It was just 'gut feeling', but I could tell they take business very seriously and I felt they would be uncomfortable on a first name basis. Everyone we have met with has been very cognizant of titles. Everything seems to be on a very formal basis so I was just trying to go along with it. You know—when in Rome,—."

Marlena added her reasoning. "Joe is right, Phil. Until a Mexican businessman gets to know you quite well and invites you to be on a first name basis, titles of respect are used. And as for me, a woman in business who is not a secretary or administrative assistant is a rarity in Mexico. People here will give me a little slack because I am an American, but I realize that I must play it pretty cool so I don't offend anyone. They will get used to me eventually, and then I can participate just as always."

"Wow! I guess I was so caught up in the conversation, I didn't pay any attention to all of that. Sorry."

Marlena reminded him, again—"Remember, everything here takes—"

"TIME—I know, I know."

CHAPTER 8
Building Credibility

At breakfast in the hotel, Bob was glancing through a local newspaper. Joe couldn't help chuckling as he approached the table. "What's going on, Bob? Did you suddenly learn to read Spanish overnight?"

"Oh sure. Give me a hard time already this morning." Bob noticed Phil and Marlena also approaching as he laughed back his retort. "I will have you know that there is a very good reason for my having this paper."

"I'm sure there is. I just can't guess what it might be at the moment."

"OK. Look at this." Bob held up a full page advertisement for the rest of the group to see. "I've been noticing a distinguishing difference between the ads here in Mexico and what I am used to in the U.S. I always have to have some noise on in the morning when I'm getting dressed, even if I don't particularly pay attention to it. So, I didn't bother to tune in to English speaking television stations; I just left on the Spanish channel. But I started to notice that the ads are different. They don't seem to be the "sound byte" style as in the U.S. The ads here are bright and flashy and noisy, just like ads anywhere, but the message seems to be more complete—even thought I don't understand the words. Our ads in the U.S. tend to be snippets of sentences a lot of the time; but I don't think that is what is going on here.

"Noticing that got me thinking about our method of advertising for CE products. Even though we do co-op advertising with our distributors, the ads are usually designed by our ad agency and then the distributors dub in their names. So—I was considering that our ads may have to be changed more than just translated into Spanish to be effective here in Mexico.—And THAT'S why I was looking at the local newspaper, to see what the style the advertising really is."

"You are on to an important point, Bob." Marlena had been listening to Bob's comments intently. "Advertising styles *are* different in Mexico than in the U.S. From what I have studied so far, the industry to industry advertising is colorful and creative, but quite 'formal'—for lack of a better word. I think it goes back to the fact that Mexican businessmen take business very personally, and therefore very seriously. Anything that makes light of their business is not particularly appreciated; so humor would have to be carefully tested before being used, or just simply avoided. Business ads don't poke fun at the company, product, or anyone else for that matter.

"Another thing we will have to consider is that newspapers in Mexico may not be the most effective media for our advertising. In the not so distant past, newspapers were truly controlled by the ruling politicians. Consequently, they only printed the news that the politicians wanted the people to read. Anything controversial was either changed or left out all together. The people knew that the papers didn't tell the real story, so they didn't bother to purchase and read the papers. SO, even though things may have improved over the last decade, the people never really got into the 'newspaper habit' as in the U.S. Other media may be more advantageous."

"What sorts of media are you thinking of, Marlena? Television is hard to target, and tends to be expensive."

"That's certainly true, Phil. CE wouldn't have to opt for television. We may want to consider radio, however. Almost everyone in Mexico—country-wide—has a radio. By selecting appropriate channels that appeal to the business market, and selecting the appropriate time slots, we could put together a pretty effective advertising campaign.

"We would also want to consider the more traditional media such as industry magazines, for advertising our products. As we discussed when we were considering purchasing mailing lists, many of the top data communications magazines have large numbers of subscribers here in Mexico. The target industries we have selected have their own magazines as well, just as in the U.S. And, of course, the various industry associations normally publish some sort of periodical.

"There are also some alternative media here that we don't have in the U.S. Did you notice the round columns, almost like kiosks, at the bus stops? They are covered in advertisements."

"I saw those." Joe had been making an extra effort to notice everything he could when the team was walking through the city. "I was even thinking how they seemed so 'European'. They aren't something I see in the U.S., now that I think about it. But—bus stops? Who would we reach in our target market at a bus stop?"

"Remember," Marlena quickly answered Joe's doubt, "people are not allowed to drive their car everyday in Mexico City. They have to alternate days of driving; so public transportation is used by most everyone. The columns have high visibility—just as placards on the buses themselves would."

"I think I can see where this is heading." Now it was Phil who interrupted. He had been putting everyone's comments together in his thoughts. "We are going to have to find a good ad agency here in Mexico and get them working with our agency back in Phoenix. Our agency is very well versed in our industry and products, so the Mexican agency wouldn't have to be expert in data communications products. They would just have to know how to create the right style, find the best cost-effective media, work with the distributors here in Mexico, and that sort of thing. The trick will be getting two very different agencies to work closely together for the benefit of Carlsbad Equipment Corp."

"We can ask our account team at our agency if they have any affiliations with Mexican agencies. Since so many of our competitors are already established here in Mexico, I will bet a lot of U.S. agencies have already crossed this bridge." As Bob was speaking, he suddenly stopped, and then began again—almost as if he were thinking aloud. "You know—we could sort of show off our wares in this situation." As everyone looked at him rather puzzled, Bob continued, "Why don't we use our own products to link our agency with the Mexican ad agency over a network? Besides proving our products can do that, it would give the agency people first hand experience in gaining the benefits of interactive design systems. We could even link in the CE design people and have a three-way interactive system. Think about it—screen sharing would allow the artists to work on a creative idea together, in real time. They wouldn't have to draw something, send it to the other group, wait for comments, re-draw it, send it again, and on and on. They could save all that time and hassle—which is especially important now that we found out the mail system here in Mexico can't be counted on. Then, with the CE advertising people on the same system, the whole ad could be finalized and approved in a fraction of the time it would otherwise take. What do you think?"

Marlena was excited about the idea. "It sounds great. I can see a couple of challenges, but we can address them. For one thing, we should be certain that we can scramble or encrypt the information on the network. I'm not sure what the U.S. government thinks of that, since we would be sending encrypted data over the public network, across the border, to a third party company—but, I will check on it when we get home. Encryption would be important since in a market this competitive, advertising information would be extraordinarily valuable to a competitor.

"The other concern may be tougher to handle.—How do we get the designers in the U.S. agency to share their ideas with another agency? They have just begun working on a team with CE. Up until very recently, their idea of "team" was just within their own walls. Well, we will have to present this as a 'new-age' idea that will bring them to the leading edge of their industry.—I'll work on that when we get home, too."

Joe added his thought to the conversation. "I really am convinced that we need a Mexican ad agency working with us. I have been wondering whether there are any legal considerations regarding advertising that are different than in the U.S. For example, is it OK to hint about a new product coming before it is really available? I have heard of some countries where you can't advertise a product until it is ready to be shipped in quantity. An agency in Mexico that knows all of the laws and regulations could certainly save us a lot of grief."

"See! Look what my scanning a local newspaper got us into." Now it was Bob who had to laugh. "Every little thing leads us to the fact that we still have a lot of homework to do. First, however, how about breakfast?"

As the group was finishing their breakfast coffee, Phil was again talking about advertising and the alternative media. "I was thinking about a way to meet two objectives, simultaneously. We have developed a pretty extensive list of potential customers from the various sources we discovered. What if we developed a direct mail mini-brochure that also contained a short but pointed survey. You know, it could be something like two pages that the person could fill out, tear off, and send in to receive some sort of a gift. We would have to make sure the survey had the right questions to provide us some insight into customer requirements, purchasing channels, network development plans, and such—and of course, it would have to be in Spanish."

Bob picked up on the idea right away. "That would be great. We could get some direct information on who are the best distributors, which customers are planning to invest in their network in the near future, what sorts of applications they are going to deploy—all kinds of information, including the basic demographics such as what industry they are in, how many locations are in their network, if they have U.S. affiliates, etc. It would really help us validate some of our research as to target industries, distribution channels, locations, training requirements, and everything— AND it would be straight from the customer without any filtering from a distributor."

Phil was beginning to think of all the benefits of such a tool. "The brochure could be fairly simple, I think. It should introduce Carlsbad Equipment Corp. more than try to sell a product. As everyone keeps telling us, the business people want to get to know the company before they will deal with us; and this could be a good introductory piece. It should talk about CE history, maybe quote some of our satisfied customers as references—maybe, it should even profile some of the CE employees—you know, make it sort of personal.

"The gift should be something pretty nice so people will send back the questionnaire. I know, what if we sent half of something, and they got the second half when they sent back the survey?"

"Or, better yet—" Bob added his thoughts since he and Phil were quite used to working together in such a brainstorming sort of style, "they could get half for sending in the questionnaire, and the selected distributor could deliver the second half at their convenience—like a locked treasure box and the distributor has the key."

"MM—hold on a minute, guys. Remember the mail system in Mexico? It doesn't work very well if you recall." Marlena figured her statement would get their attention. "Direct mail isn't very effective in Mexico—especially if you can't be certain that it will get through in a timely manner.

"But that isn't the biggest concern I have with your idea. Direct mail surveys from strangers are simply anti-cultural in Mexico. The introductory brochure, without the questionnaire, may not be a bad idea, but not sent through the mail. Even though the people are anxious to expand their technological base according to all indications, keep in mind that Mexican people are very private—about themselves, and about their business. They just are not going to divulge all sorts of information on a form and send it to some unknown person in an unknown company.

"We are going to have to be rather creative about the research and advertising tools we use. The things we have gotten used to in the U.S. just aren't done here. Phone surveys would be impossible. Although they may be very polite, they wouldn't tell the surveyor anything. Telemarketing is not prevalent in Mexico. At the residential level, of course, not enough homes have telephones to make it worthwhile; and at the business level, people don't want to give out information or take the time away from their business. Focus groups for research are also difficult in Mexico. It just simply is not comfortable for a Mexican businessman to express his opinions about something new in a room full of strangers."

Phil was trying not to get irritated. "Gees, Marlena! What will work?"

"The things we have talked about before. Working through the associations, the Chambers, the U.S. customers that have affiliates, and Sr. Guererra to get introduced and make personal contact with people will get things started. Surveying will have to be done one on one, and when the Mexican businessman feels comfortable—not in the first or second meeting. Carlsbad Equipment Corp.—*and* Phil Sierra- both have to gain some credibility here first.

"Most business people and especially government people want to see demonstrations of products and services. They do want catalogs and brochures, and those have to be informative and fairly detailed—from everything I have seen so far. Think of the 'good ol' days' in the U.S. when people went to the neighborhood store where they knew the store owner and he knew them. They could tell the store owner what special things they needed, and he would get those things to meet the needs of his customers and because he considered most of them his friends. Advertising in those days might be an ad in the paper or a sign in the window—but it was credible because the people trusted the store owner who ran the ad, not the ad itself. That's the kind of advertising and selling that people still expect here in Mexico. For their personal goods, many people here still have those shops in their neighborhoods—and, they expect their business needs to be met in much the same way.— Actually, there is something very alluring about getting the personal touch back into business and dealing with people you know and trust, don't you think?"

At this point Joe, who had been taking the whole conversation in quietly, offered his thinking to the group. "I believe you are right, Marlena, about the allure of personal one to one business; and I think we can creatively combine that with some of the new technologies as well. A lot of companies have been putting servers onto the Internet. With the World Wide Web now available, Internet users can find the 'Home Page' of the company and gain information about the company and the products without feeling under pressure of having a salesman call on them. Then, when they find something interesting, they can enter a query about the products, services, training, or whatever directly to the company. Someone in the company can personally answer the query and begin a dialog. Although people on the Internet really get incensed if someone actually tries to sell something over the net, they don't mind at all if a company will share information. Ultimately the dialog could result in a qualified customer for a distributor.

"To do something like that, it means that CE would have to staff an Internet line with someone who could answer the queries, qualify the lead, carry on the dialog, and finally introduce the customer to the distributor—and, of course, follow up to see that the distributor met the customer's requirement. It would be a low key, 'non-salesy', internal sales desk that provided the customer with a personal contact. It's a 'virtual store owner' in your scenario, Marlena; someone who could listen to the customer's needs, make recommendations, and be an on-line friend."

"That's not a bad idea, Joe. I wonder how extensively the Internet World Wide Web has spread into Mexico." Marlena was considering the potential staffing requirements for answering queries about CE in Spanish.

"I just might have some information about that very thing." Phil was amazed at how each of the team members often were thinking along the same lines and collecting information that supported each others' ideas. "I happened to see a magazine at the hotel called *"TelePress—Latinoamerica"* . Even though it is mostly in Spanish, I could recognize that the headline on the cover was about the Internet. I bought it hoping to ask Marlena to check it out later today."

"Well, how about that. Let's take a look at it." Marlena was glad to be able to address the team's question right away. "This first article, "Latin America is 'Internetting'", tells that the number of users of the

Internet grows 15% per month, with about 40 million users on line in 146 countries. At the end of this year, they expect about 100 million users. The people of Latin America don't want to be left behind, and the demand in Latin America has caused the installation of thousands of kilometers of fiber optics in the past two years. The article goes on to discuss the origination of the Internet and its evolution of services. It explains that previously, only the giant companies could manage to communicate electronically world-wide on their own private networks; but now, thanks to the Internet, the level of competition is more or less equal between small, medium, and large companies. And it even mentions your point, Joe—that an export business can place its catalog in a virtual showcase on the net for clients around the world to see. The article cautions that people can't actually pay for products over the Internet because a hacker could get the credit card number and use it later; however, a California company is working on that issue so this author expects that in five years the major part of business transactions will be via the Internet.

"That point leads into the authors second article, *"The Financial World and the Internet"*, about J. P. Morgan company using the Internet even though it has one of the best private financial networks in the world. Morgan has put up a gateway to the Internet. One of the key services they use it for is to communicate with their vendors of hardware and software for support. What used to take a couple of days to contact the support people, ship a diskette of software to identify the problem, and finally get an answer, now can sometimes be completed via the Internet in a few minutes. The Morgan person can attach a document or software with the message and get an answer right away."

Joe was quickly thinking about expanded use of the Internet. "We could provide distributor support and training that way too. What else does the article say, Marlena?"

"Let's see—Morgan uses the Internet for research also, such as accessing the public files of the SEC and then formats the files for various users in the organization. Basically, this article gives good examples as to how the Internet could be used, even if the financial company has its own network—like Banamex.

"Oh, here is the information about the California company working on creating financial transactions over the Internet—"First Virtual Holdings". For right now, First Virtual registers clients' credit card numbers and acts as a broker between them and businesses who list products on the Internet. Basically, they are ensuring the businesses that the clients and the requests are valid, and facilitating payment for the clients.

"Another article here speaks to the enormous demand for Internet services in Mexico. It is titled, *"Mexico Awaits Regularization"*. Mexico has new telecommunications regulations to try to ensure the interoperability of networks and fair competition of network service providers. We probably need to make certain we and our distributors stay on top of those new regulations."

"Man, I would say so! Oh, notice in the back of that magazine, it lists upcoming events." Phil pointed to the back as Marlena started to hand him the magazine. "I was thinking it would be good for us to attend a data communications oriented trade show here in Mexico. You know, we should check out not only who is showing, but how the show looks and operates. If advertising has a different style, I'll bet there are differences in how products are displayed and such. Maybe our next trip could be at the time there is a trade show, and we could see for ourselves."

"Great idea, Phil! But for now, we had better head for the airport, and plan the next trip on our way home from this one."

Several weeks later, Bob stopped by to wish Phil a good trip back to Mexico. "I really wish I were going with you guys. I think you are going to learn a lot at this show and I wish I could go along; but you know how it is—once in awhile family obligations just can't be maneuvered out of the way."

"Hey, no problem, Bob. You can be certain that we will fill you in with the finest detail, *ad nauseam* , when we get back." Phil was thinking about the upcoming weekend. "I'm really glad Marlena suggested that we go down a few days early. Since the trade show starts on September 19th, we can go down ahead of the show and be there for the September 16th, Mexican Independence Day celebrations. That should be exciting."

"Now, you said the show is in Mexico City even though it is called 'Representaciones Guadalajara' right?"

Phil pulled out his itinerary and looked at the details. "Right. The trade show highlights Guadalajara, but is held at the U.S. Trade Center in Mexico City. It sounds like a pretty large show—over 250 exhibitors."

"Well, like I said, I wish I could go—Just be careful, OK? Remember what Marlena told us. September 16th marks the *beginning* of the revolution to gain independence from Spain. The priest, Father Hidalgo, began the fight with a small group that eventually amassed into a group of over 60,000 people a month later. But it was really the battle near Guadalajara that was his defeat; after which, he was beheaded. It was eleven years later, in 1821, that Mexico really became an independent nation."

"Bob, I recall the story, but I think you are trying to make another point, right?"

"Well, Phil, just keep in mind what Marlena said. Mexico is quite advanced, but it is still an emerging nation—politically and economically. This trade show highlights Guadalajara, and Father Hidalgo was defeated near Guadalajara. There are still some revolutionary groups in Mexico who could take the opportunity of Independence Day to make their point, trying for another *beginning,* so to speak—so just don't be careless."

"I appreciate your concern, Bob—and I try never to be careless. Remember what else Marlena said. Even the revolutionary groups who want faster political reform recognize Mexico's need for international business and foreign investment to accelerate her growth and help make a better living for everyone. That one particular revolutionary leader writes some pretty savvy and inspiring letters to the newspapers. He isn't going to jeopardize important opportunities for his country. Besides, a revolutionary leader's popularity would quickly drop off if investment slow-downs and a consequent economic depression become directly attributable to the revolutionary's actions. Marlena emphasized that we don't have to be paranoid—just take the same precautions as in any big city. I'm sure it isn't any more dangerous than New York."

"I'm sure you're right. And it will be a wonderful time to see the celebrations and fiestas—the costumed dancers are so colorful and the music is so upbeat and happy—Boy, I do wish I were going with you. Well, *buen viaje* !"

As Phil, Joe, and Marlena entered the trade show floor, they were astounded by the displays and sounds of so many exhibitors. Phil suggested they split up to make the best use of their time. "We can compare what we have seen this evening at dinner. If you get the chance, besides checking out what the competition is showing and who is looking, see if you can talk with some of the show organizers for the various companies. We can learn a lot from other people's experiences before we try to exhibit at such a show ourselves."

That evening at dinner, everyone was excited about what they had seen and heard. Joe was explaining his observation. "It reminded me of the auto shows I used to go to with my dad when I was a kid—you know—a lot of 'flash', sort of carnival-like—and, wow, all the pretty girls working the exhibits. The American companies exhibits looked very conservative, didn't they? You could really spot the difference at a glance."

"Yeah, that's for sure. I spoke with one fellow about give-aways. He said they keep the show give-aways pretty inexpensive. The attendees aren't necessarily qualified clients, and just like in the U.S., a lot of people just collect the freebies because they are free. But he said that for their Mexican customers and distributors, they have created a special crystal vase with a design in it that indicates a true partnership between the countries and the companies. He told me that a symbolic gift that demonstrates the partnership commitment is really appreciated. His company considers it a very important gesture. The gift isn't very expensive—just thoughtful; and every recipient has displayed it proudly in their company offices."

"What a great idea! I spoke with one company that I think is heading into trouble, but I knew they weren't looking for comment from me." Marlena aroused the curiosity of both Phil and Joe with her statement. "This company is planning a special evening for their biggest distributors—a big dinner and live entertainment for all the employees and their spouses. The problem is that in Mexico you just can't do something special for your big customers and not include the rest of your customers as well. When you do that, you offend both the ones invited and the ones not invited because you are indicating that you are not interested in the small companies—that you don't consider them equally important. Once again people forget that business in Mexico is taken personally, and leaving the smaller customers out would be a personal affront. The ones who are invited will be uncomfortable taking part in the event; and I'll bet that some will even decline the invitation. This company would be much better off doing something on a less grand scale and making it an open invitation for all their customers—those who want to come, can; and those who don't, can simply decline without any embarrassment."

"Ouch! That's a tough lesson to learn the hard way." Phil was recalling a conversation he also had during the day. "It's interesting that even competitors such as you are talking about—the big and little distributors of the same company's products—would be offended if the other guy is left out. That emphasizes an incredible story another fellow told me. This company asked for price quotations from freight companies for shipping the booth display, equipment, literature, etc. down here for the show. The guy told me that they initially received three quotes. However, one company withdrew theirs when they found out who else had quoted. When he asked some people why the one withdrew, he was told that they didn't want to compete with friends. That company would rather this job went to the other company, and they would quote on a different job another time. I've never experienced anything like that; and from the amazed look on this guy's face as he told me about it, I'd guess he never had either. I can't decide whether I like that practice or not. On one hand, it smacks of collusion and price fixing; but I don't think that is how it is intended. It really is looking out for each other; and on the other hand, helping each other stay in business can be appealing. I'm going to have to think about this custom some more."

Marlena had to laugh at Phil's perplexed look. "You don't have to judge another culture or customs, Phil. You just have to be aware of the differences from your own so you can know what to expect.

"That reminds me of another point. One company apparently had a little difficulty getting some of their equipment through. The Mexican government is really trying to crack down on any sort of 'extra payment' requirements, but a few people still try it and get away with it. In this case, the amount requested was fairly nominal, and the truck driver made a judgment call and paid the fee in order to get the equipment to the show in time for set up. However, it raises the point that Carlsbad Equipment Corp. will have to be very explicit about our policy against bribery or extraneous payments of any kind. Once we can get our reputation established as only dealing above board and not giving in to pressures for bribes, the problem will dwindle away. If a strict policy is upheld, it makes it easier for our employees and distributors because they can always use the policy as an excuse for not paying. When the requesting party recognizes that the person may really lose his job or his business for paying 'extra payments' they tend to stop asking. We need to think of an effective way to communicate our policy right off the bat."

"Good point! I ran into a fellow who was perplexed by a problem of a different sort." Joe was trying to recall the man's exact words in order to describe the situation. "It seems that although he was on site and constantly talking to the contractor who was setting up the booth, he didn't find out until almost the opening hour that the lighting wasn't working properly. He kept asking me, 'Why didn't they tell me,—we could have fixed this two days ago!'"

Marlena thought about the problem for a moment. "It's HOW someone asks the questions that is important. When you notice the interaction among the workers and their supervisors, you can see a lot of emotional talking and gesturing—a lot of 'dressing down'—; but the supervisor is careful that he never personally humiliates the worker. It is more like a parent/child relationship."

"Oh—I remember hearing a little about that. I was told that Mexican workers would take failure to expertly perform very personally, so a supervisor must be sure to emphasize that it was the *thing* not the person that failed. This man should have concentrated his questions around the lighting and what it was doing wrong, not on how it was installed or shipped, or on who did what."

"Exactly, Joe. You have to ask the questions in the right way to get the information. The workers take personal pride in what they do, so you just cannot be perceived as attacking them or their work. You must ask questions about how the things are performing. Ha Ha, we have to get used to asking what an inanimate object did today. Have you noticed the people taking pictures of the booths they have worked on? They are very proud of their work. They really care, and you certainly don't want to insult or destroy that special interest."

"Wow, this is all going to take a lot of practice, and a different mind-set—about trade shows, advertising, asking questions, handling people, etc. etc. Wait until we tell Bob everything we have been finding out. He will never believe it." Phil had to laugh to himself as he pictured Bob's face at the next team meeting.

CHAPTER 9

Price and Pesos

Finally the day arrived that the team had been anticipating with excitement. Phil, his wife Mary, Joe, his wife Sarah, and Sr. Guererra met at the airport. Sr. Guererra had been at the Board meeting that approved the key objectives of the new CE venture in Mexico. This was to be a dual purpose trip. Carlsbad Equipment Corp. was going to contractually sign their first Mexican distributor; and the Sierras and Tricots were going to tour the area to investigate potential housing. CE and the team had determined that Phil and Joe would move to Mexico City to get the branch office opened, the distributors started, and CE established in the new market. Once they had found homes and relocated, they would stay for three years.

The team had had long discussions regarding the best strategy to support the new venture. They determined that to avoid the situation in which the branch became too separate and independent or too centralized by headquarters control, Marlena and Bob would stay in Phoenix to be the branch representatives and support on a daily basis in the normal operations of Carlsbad Equipment. In this way, the branch could operate somewhat independently but still be closely linked to the CE functions and strategies. When the team's recommendations had been presented to Paul Esters the CEO, and the Board, everyone fully supported the idea. Mr. Esters was very pleased with the idea of incorporating all that the team had learned into the daily operations through the contribution of Marlena and Bob, and still being able to capitalize on the strengths of Phil and Joe to open the new business in Mexico.

Arthur Smith, the CE finance specialist who worked on partnerships and alliances was also going on this trip to assist with the contract details between CE and the new distributor.

"Phil, how long do you think we will have to stay down there?" Arthur had packed one small suitcase full of bottled water and was calculating how many days his supply would last. "It's awfully hot there this time of year, isn't it? I just don't want to drag out these negotiations any longer than we have to."

Phil was surprised at Arthur's obvious nervousness. "Hot down there? For goodness sake, Arthur, you live in Phoenix, Arizona. How hot is hot?" Everyone including Arthur laughed at the comment; but Phil was concerned about how uncomfortable Arthur seemed.

The next morning in Mexico City, Phil and Mary rose early to take a walk around the central part of the city. "If you stand here, you can get a terrific view of that special mural by Diego Rivera I was telling you about. Isn't that something? Rivera was actually contracted by Rockefeller to paint a mural in New York. But—after all that work, when it was all done, Rockefeller had it destroyed because Rivera had included the face of Lenin in it. Rivera was a political activist in Mexico, and a great fan of Lenin. I can sort of understand why Rocky had it destroyed—and still, all that work! Those were really heavy times, weren't they?"

"I'm glad they were before my time," Mary had to smile at Phil's excitement that was obviously partly based on his desire for her to like their soon-to-be new home. "The city is so huge that I have to admit it scares me a little. But—I do think this will be a wonderful experience for all of us, especially the kids. All of this history, and the different culture, and the different language comes alive when you are actually here. It will be a geography lesson they will never forget."

Phil laughed, "I just can't wait to see the expressions on their faces when they first take it all in. Of course John was acting a little less than enthused about leaving his friends until I mentioned that we could take our vacations at some of the most famous beaches in this hemisphere. I think he will have some adjusting to do for awhile, but in the long run what he can learn here will serve him well in whatever he decides to do.

"Well, we had better get back. Sr. Guererra has arranged a tour guide for you and Sarah. The rest of us will have to get over to the distributor's and see if we can get this deal put together."

When the Carlsbad Equipment Corp. group arrived at the distributor's they were cordially guided into a small conference room where coffee was awaiting them. Sr. Leo Montecino Martinez, the owner of the distributorship and Sr. Alberto Ernesto Leon, the attorney joined the others almost immediately. Arthur and Alberto were introduced. Phil and Joe had met Leo Montecino several times before and had had numerous telephone conversations prior to this contract meeting. Sr. Montecino opened the conversation. "Mr. Sierra, did your wife accompany you on this trip as you had planned?"

"Yes, indeed. Mrs. Tricot has also come this time. Sr. Guererra graciously arranged a tour of the city for them this morning—to help them get a feeling of Mexico."

"Magnificent! My friend Paco Guererra Montemayor is a generous host. They will enjoy their morning." Sr. Montecino smiled broadly and seemed genuinely relieved that Phil's and Joe's wives would have an enjoyable day.

"Well, let's get started." Arthur was still anxious to get underway in order to finish as soon as possible. He felt it was important to set the stage in CE's favor at the very beginning. "I think that Carlsbad Equipment Corp. is the one taking most of the risk here. With the tremendous peso devaluation and capital flight out of Mexico, the economy in Mexico is certainly rocky, to say the least. Everyone is expecting rampant inflation to take off, and interest rates to be too high to enable most small businesses to borrow any money to purchase capital equipment. So, CE will be taking a very cautious approach to this whole venture."

The faces of both Phil and Leo Montecino turned very red. It was Joe who interrupted. "Arthur, I suspect that both Sr. Montecino and Sr. Ernesto Leon know the details of the economic situation here much better than we do. Perhaps it would be better if you spoke of the things we know very well. For instance, the fact is that Carlsbad Equipment Corp. is looking at this partnership to be a very long term commitment. CE is not expecting short term financial benefits; rather, we expect to build a long term relationship that will expand our market and create many benefits, financial and others, for years to come. We have certainly noticed the trends in Mexico toward true political stability, privatization of most companies, major infrastructure investments, improved shipping transportation, and the total commitment to stable growth. CE would like to be a part of all of this, and hopefully make a significant contribution in the process.

"I think the 'pacto' between the government, industry, and the unions that makes a joint commitment to hold down prices and wage levels is a strong indicator that all of Mexico is working toward growth and stability. Any business venture has a little risk. CE is proud to be a joint marketing partner with *datared* ; and we are looking forward to the excitement of growing this business."

Phil was relieved that Joe had taken command of the situation and had squelched Arthur's posturing. He suddenly realized Arthur's opening, which would have been a very normal negotiating tactic in the U.S., was very uncomfortable for both parties here in Mexico.

Once underway, the discussions continued throughout the day. The lunch was shorter than normal; and the group continued working until late in the evening. Having a few key points left to agree, the group decided to adjourn and meet again in the morning. As the trio reached the hotel, Phil felt the need to counsel Arthur a bit. "Arthur, I know you have negotiated many distributor arrangements for CE—and you are very good at what you do. But, this is a new venture for us, and to a degree for Sr. Montecino as well. After all, although he is a distributor for two other U.S. companies, he doesn't know us any better than we know him. Partnerships like this are based on trust here. Both sides have to be able to count on the other party to help work through details and difficulties as they arise. We can't build every possible situation into a contract. What we need is a structured process that lets us work together with some flexibility to smooth out the rough spots as they occur. Can't you back off a little?"

Arthur had been losing his patience as the day had worn on. "Phil, you say that now. But if CE starts losing big bucks in this arrangement, you will be very glad if I have managed to get all the possible events covered in this contract. I'll see you in the morning."

As Arthur walked away, Phil turned to Joe. "I think he is approaching this whole negotiation the wrong way. Still, he has a point. If things go sour, we need some sort of recourse."

"I don't think the problem is what he is putting into the contract; it is *how* he is putting things into the contract. It is clear that Arthur doesn't trust anybody here and really feels that we are doing *datared* a big favor 'letting' them distribute for us. Maybe we can find out what is driving his attitude at breakfast before the meeting." Joe headed for his room. "Get some sleep, Phil. It will get easier tomorrow—it has to."

The next morning's breakfast discussion between Phil, Joe, and Arthur had been somewhat agitated. Arthur was struggling with the whole process. "These people are driving me crazy. We can't get closure on any one point before they jump all over the map to bring up everything else. Look at this check-list. I only have one thing checked off—everything else is still in negotiation. I have never been in a contract meeting like this. Usually, both parties agree to the key items to be discussed and we can proceed in an orderly fashion to address each item. This has been a free-for-all, so far."

"They have a different way of processing through such things, Arthur." Phil was beginning to see how difficult this was for Arthur. "It is just a different way of thinking about things—we will all get to the same conclusions. In the U.S., we tend to take things very linearly—left to right, top to bottom—in a very logical fashion. Here, things are considered much more holistically. How one decision may impact something else that to us seems totally unrelated is very important to the Mexican business people. We need to provide the time to work through all the points and try to see the total picture from their perspective. Some times they will revisit a point several times because a new item may impact the point already considered decided. It is important that we talk through the various elements of the contract, just as you pointed out. But it isn't as important in what order the elements are discussed. I suspect that what will happen is that your checklist will stay open until almost everything is decided—and then, you will check everything off simultaneously. What do you think?"

"Well, you had better be right. I guess I don't have to like these people or their way of thinking. I just have to get a good deal."
Arthur's retort infuriated Phil at first; however, as he thought about it, it deeply concerned him. Arthur's inflexibility and total cultural insensitivity could jeopardize the entire venture. At the lunch break that day, Phil returned with Arthur to the hotel while Joe met Mary and Sarah for lunch. "Arthur, I know this has been a strain on you, and that you have an awful lot of work that has to be done before deadline back in Phoenix. I remember your comment that you didn't want to drag these negotiations out. I think that between Joe and I, we will be able to bring this deal to closure. You have raised all of the issues, and we know the CE position. Now it will just take time to talk it all through. Why don't you go ahead and head back this afternoon. We will finish up here."

"Phil, are you sure you can handle this by yourself? That is taking on a big responsibility."

"It's OK, Arthur. Joe and I will work it together so neither of us forgets any of the elements. You head on home; and thank you."

Before going back to the contract meeting, Phil called Marlena to give her an update on the progress so far. Marlena included Bob so that the whole team would have all the same information simultaneously. Phil had explained the situation with Arthur. Bob could tell his long-time friend was somewhat upset.

"Phil, I was a little worried about Arthur being assigned to put this deal together in the first place. Professionally, he is a top notch financial wizard and has negotiated some terrific deals for CE before. The only thing is, I don't know that Arthur has ever done much traveling around even the U.S., much less outside the country. And most of his contact with Mexican people has been with the gardeners and the pool service people around his house. He seems to mostly stick with people of his own kind—which is OK, I guess, but it doesn't prepare a person very well for interacting with different cultures and places. For a week before you guys left, Arthur must have asked me three times whether I had gotten sick on the food or water while I was in Mexico. He seem sort of obsessed with that."

Marlena added her thoughts as well. "Excessive concern about safety, or health matters, or how to get around in a different country, etc. are sort of classic symptoms of culture shock. I have heard of people almost starving themselves because they can't get adjusted to the differences and the most obvious difference is the food—although that is just the tip of their fears. For some people, culture shock can become a serious problem.

"In any case, Phil, I think you made the right call. If Arthur has identified all of the issues that must be negotiated, then he has already performed a great service for us. You and Joe can bring those issues to closure. Besides, you and Joe were coached along with Arthur by the special attorney that CE's legal group brought in as an expert on international contracts, right? She seemed to really understand Mexican law and the possible pitfalls.

"Anyway, I don't think Arthur had a complete picture of CE's objectives for opening the Mexican market. I just received a new report from the Conference Board about the North American Outlook. It considers the economic forecast for Canada, Mexico, and the U.S., reviews some of the statistics since NAFTA was passed, and most important speaks to the trend in partnerships and alliances. The report pointed out that one of the difficulties in structuring successful alliances seems to be the unspoken and often unrecognized difference in the objectives of the alliance partners. Most of the U.S. companies seem to be seeking the financial benefits of entering the new market to increase volume and gain economies of scale. The Mexican business partners, on the other hand, are particularly looking for ways to diversify their product lines and gain access to technological know-how through their U.S. partner. It would seem that both sets of objectives would complement each other, but sometimes the emphasis put on one or the other objective causes one of the potential partners to back out.

"It sounds as if that could have happened to us if Arthur pushed his perspective too hard. As you said, this first deal is a learning experience for all of us, so we need to understand all of the objectives and perspectives of all the parties involved. Sr. Montecino seems to be a very solid company owner; and with all the checking Sr. Guererra did for us on *datared's* debt structure, receivables, service reputation, customer base, financial history, and so on, we should really be at less risk than with some of the U.S. distributors who haven't been checked out half as much. Besides, the final signature won't go on the contract until that consulting attorney reviews the whole deal, remember?"

"Well, I appreciate your points of view. Thanks for the counsel. I had better get back to the meeting. We are going to try to finalize the pricing structure this afternoon."

After a long afternoon and evening of discussion, Phil and Joe were finally getting back to the hotel. Joe was still in amazement over the afternoon's negotiating. "Man o'man! I thought I was at the street market in New Delhi there for awhile. I haven't seen such price haggling since—well, ever—I guess." Joe started laughing. "Sr. Montecino was getting such enjoyment out of it. When I think of it, he had sort of hinted that he felt Alberto Ernesto Leon was one of the best negotiators he had ever met. Now I know what he meant. Every time Alberto would counter with another pricing offer, I watched Sr. Montecino's eyes light up. They were really having fun."

Phil was laughing now, too. "I think Sr. Guererra must have figured we would get to pricing this afternoon, because he sure showed up at the right time. He seemed pleasantly surprised, however, that we were holding our own in the process."

"Yeah, it seemed as if we gained some true credibility. They could tell that we had done our homework. The pricing structure we proposed was well thought out and based on solid reasoning. Each time we explained our points and why we couldn't agree to the concessions they requested, they ended up supporting our position."

"I think we teamed well, too—you would make a point and I gave an explanation, and then vice versa—and Sr. Guererra seemed to know exactly when to support us to end the haggling on a particular detail." Phil was replaying the discussion in his mind. "I think everyone was really impressed with your explanation of gray marketing that has to be avoided—how we want to price aggressively to quickly penetrate the market, but that we have to be careful that U.S. dealers who are not licensed to carry CE equipment won't start raiding Mexican distributors, buying at the lower prices and reselling in the U.S. market. They could see our predicament and were truly willing to help us avoid that problem."

"True, but I think what made Sr. Montecino the happiest was your offer to split any losses with him that are due to peso exchange rate shifts. That helped him believe that we are willing to share his risk to help grow his business. Did you notice that the haggling basically stopped after that?"

"As a matter of fact, Joe, now that you mention it—right after that, Sr. Ernesto Leon accepted our request that they take possession of the equipment at the bridge and bring it across as the importer for no price concessions or fee for extra freight. That little detail will save us significant cost and effort."

Joe was laughing again, "And a good day was had by all! So, let's pick up Sarah and Mary and celebrate with a special dinner at that restaurant they have been wanting to try."

"Right. Besides, we have to tell them that they will be going back tomorrow alone since Sr. Guererra has arranged for you and I to meet with the senior economist in the President's advisory committee. That will be a fascinating meeting tomorrow. I am really looking forward to it."

The next morning, Phil and Joe accompanied Mary and Sarah to the airport and waited while they boarded the airplane. They then went straight to the office of the senior economist and arrived twenty minutes ahead of Sr. Guererra. Paco Guererra smiled at Phil's eagerness for this meeting. "Buenos dias, Sr. Guererra. We thought we would try to arrive a little early just in case we would get caught in traffic."

"Buenos dias, Sr. Sierra and Sr. Tricot. It is good to see you this morning. Let us proceed, please."

When they entered the office, Sr. Guererra approached the secretary to announce their arrival and spoke with her for several minutes in Spanish. As he came back to Phil and Joe, he had a disappointed look on his face.

"I am so sorry, gentlemen. He is not here."

Since Phil had gotten somewhat used to the different value that Mexican businessmen placed on time and promptness, he assumed the economist would arrive shortly—whenever he finished the conversation he was having somewhere else. "That's OK. We can wait. This is our only meeting today."

"No no, Sr. Sierra. He will not be here at all today. It seems that as Sr. Velasquez was speaking with me yesterday, he had forgotten that today is his grandmother's eighty-fifth birthday. The whole family is gathering for a grand fiesta in her honor; and of course, he could not miss such an occasion."

Phil was visibly irritated. "You are kidding! We postpone our flights, lose our discounted rates, take another day away from work,—AND, by the way, send *our* families on without us—and then he cancels a business meeting for a birthday party!? Why couldn't he meet with us first and go to the party this afternoon? This is truly incredible!—As a matter of fact, are you sure that he really went to a birthday party, or he just didn't feel we were important and wanted to get out of the meeting?"

"No, no Sr. Sierra. His grandmother lives in the small town of Mesa Rojo, a two hour drive from here. He had to leave very early this morning to preside over the festivities as the eldest grandson."

Joe interrupted, "Phil, calm down. I am sure that Sr. Velasquez is exactly where his secretary said he is. Remember when Marlena kept telling us that in Mexico, family is first and foremost in importance. Family obligations are extremely important—and helping family members takes precedence over business matters. Do you recall when I was upset because in the middle of a meeting Sr. Xavier interrupted our conversation to take a call from his cousin? I could understand an emergency call from his wife or children, but some casual call from a cousin—I was insulted until Marlena explained, again, that family is the most important thing here in Mexico, and that a Mexican family encompasses more than just the husband, wife, and 2.3 children in a U.S. nuclear family."

"You're right, of course, Joe. I apologize, Sr. Guererra. I am sorry that these things bother me. Sometimes some of these situations are just incredible to me. Over time, I will get used to it. Another thing our co-worker Marlena keeps reminding us of is that everything takes time."

"Of course, of course. Perhaps you will let me make this inconvenience up to you by allowing me to be your host this evening. I know a very special restaurant you will enjoy—where the food, the service, and the music is the best there is. If you will join me, I will pick you up at 8:00 this evening?."

"We would be honored and delighted, Sr. Guererra. Thank you."

When Sr. Guererra dropped Phil and Joe off at their hotel, they were discussing what to do with the suddenly free day. They now had the opportunity to visit museums, parks, various shopping districts, gardens, and so many things, they were having a hard time deciding. Joe had a twinkle in his eye, "Of course, we could spend the day reviewing the paper work from the past few days of negotiating, and go over to the U.S. Dept. of Commerce to do some checking of the competition."

Phil laughed, "That's true, we could. Well,—I vote for Chapultepec Park—what do you say?"

Later that afternoon, as they were walking through the park, Joe began a new conversation. "Phil, have you given any thought to the possibility of Carlsbad Equipment Corp. opening a maquiladora? We could put one in Agua Prieta, close enough to Bisbee to support it from our existing plant."

"Actually, the thought has crossed my mind. With all that is happening to open the branch office, find the right distributors, look for attorney's, ad agencies, shippers, financiers, etc. who understand Mexico, I haven't spent much time contemplating it. What is your thinking?"

"I can see some real benefits, I think. We know we will be manufacturing a different cabinet and repackaging the equipment. Why not do that in a maquila here in Mexico. Soon, companies will be able to sell 100% of the maquila output into Mexico. I think it will facilitate things like compliance, shipping, and I don't know what all. It seems to me we ought to look into it."

"Hum, I think you are right. We need to examine the possibility. That would be a pretty big step for CE. I have looked at the labor laws a little, regarding our branch office; and they are quite different than we are used to. The Mexican Federal Law assumes that when a worker begins doing a job for someone, that is a permanent relationship unless it is specifically spelled out in writing that it is temporary. There are things like mandatory Christmas bonuses of at least a month's pay. They have something like 12 legal holidays, and usually a week off at Easter.

"Also, we would have to check into the impact on maquiladoras with the planned evolution of the NAFTA that basically eliminates tariffs and opens truck shipping across the borders by 1997. I'll bet the Dept. of Commerce could help us get information about that.—And there is the question of whether CE would actually purchase land and facilities in Mexico, or lease. There's lots of questions as you think about that for a minute. Well, our team is still in place—just spreading out a bit. Let's start the research process next week when we get back in Phoenix."

"OK, great! Here is Tamayo's art museum. Let's do it."

Later in the evening, after a superb dinner, Phil, Joe, and Paco Guererra were recapping the last few months activities. "I am very proud to be associated with Carlsbad Equipment Corp. You have all done very fine work in preparing for your new venture in Mexico. Please know that I will be very happy to assist you and your families in any way that I can as you become established here in my country."

Both Phil and Joe were proud of themselves and their team, and excited about the future prospects. Both had come to sincerely like and deeply respect their new friend and mentor, Paco Guererra. Phil raised his glass of wine, "Thank you, Sr. Here is to an exciting and bright future with good business, and most important, good friends." Then he laughed, "With your help, Sr. Guererra, we are going to make it."

Both Joe and Paco quickly answered in unison, "We are definitely going to make it!"

CHAPTER 10
Summary

The following Spring, Phil Sierra was asked to speak at a special program hosted by the Phoenix Chamber of Commerce. The program was intended for an audience of people from small and medium businesses and was to provide practical information and advice on starting business in Mexico. Representing Carlsbad Equipment Corp., Phil was the featured dinner speaker, and he wanted to share with these people some of the key pieces of information and knowledge he had gained from his experiences of starting an operation in Mexico. He wanted people to know that it can be a very successful and rewarding venture to undertake. However, he didn't want to make everything seem overly simple. Phil had now been at this process for over a year and had lived in Mexico running the day to day operations for nearly six months; yet, everyday he was learning something new—moving, and shifting, and changing the original marketing strategy with events that still usually catch him by surprise. What can he give this audience that will be important for them to know, without overwhelming them in the 45 minutes he had been allotted?

Phil decided to begin his talk with the business and organizational aspects of U.S. / Mexican ventures and then speak to some of the cultural aspects he has learned. He opened with a reference to the Conference Board's "North American Outlook" report.

"According to a survey conducted by the Conference Board, U.S. and Canadian companies that have tried alliances and ventures in Mexico think that extraordinary changes in the market environment are the main reason alliances fail. The Mexican respondents, however, also consider partner problems and an overestimation of the market as equal elements for failure. Interestingly, all three—U.S., Canadian, and

Mexican—groups of business people list cultural differences as a key reason that otherwise sound alliances ultimately fail. How can you avoid some of these known pitfalls?

"My first word of advice is *manage expectations*—of all parties involved. You must be certain that the goals and objectives that you set for your venture into Mexico align with, and more important, support your overall company goals. You must be sure that your top management—whether that is the president of the company, the board of directors, or the financing agents—is absolutely behind the venture. When the going gets tough—and it will—you have to be able to know that your management is in this venture for the long term. Only then, can you relieve your Mexican partner's fears and distrust, and make the long term commitment that you must in order to be successful.

"Be completely aware that you cannot go into a venture in Mexico, or any emerging market, intending to reap short term profit. We in the U.S. still have a quarter by quarter view; but an investment in Mexican business must be considered a long term strategic investment. Today Coca Cola says it is reaping major international profits from investments made in emerging markets 15-20 years ago. I'm not saying everything will take 15 years before you see a payback; but I am saying to expect that financial returns will take time. Manage your company's expectations.

"As a matter of fact, give yourself more than ample time for any transaction when doing business in Mexico. Last minute details and fast contracts just won't work. It takes time to build the relationships that are so critical to get things moving. It takes time to get all approvals you will need for everything. It takes time to do your research and properly plan your business. And it takes lots of time to get all of the paperwork you need filled out. Believe me, there are no short cuts for that. Make your time estimate and then double it. Even with the much more open access because of the NAFTA, the paperwork required by two governments, banks, and multiple companies involved in contracts and sales is enormous. But most important, it takes time to get to know people—and for them to really get to know you. Be sure to give yourself enough time for that. Not only is getting to know people essential for business transactions, it makes the whole experience so much more delightful.

"And you can expect that the people you will have the opportunity to know will be very bright and sophisticated. They are sincere, highly educated, hard-working people with the exuberance and enthusiasm that comes with being energized by rapid growth, too many opportunities, and of course, a very youthful population that keeps things jumping.

"When you have developed your plan and ensured your strategy supports the overall company goals, go back and make certain that you have put check points in place to monitor the success of your marketing strategy. Now the question is, 'What constitutes success?' Success cannot be just the financial measurements when you are dealing with an emerging market, as I mentioned before. Find the things that measure your advancement toward meeting those overall company goals. Were you looking for ways to gain global market share, to increase capacity utilization, smooth out seasonality in your product line? What goals did your Mexican partner establish. Are you meeting those objectives.?

"Then, when you have built in the check points, be certain to build in the flexibility you will need. When the measurements indicate something has to be changed, be able to change it. Don't let people or established systems lock in a strategy that can't be adjusted to the market.

"On the other hand, recognize that it is not possible to implement a strategy that never solidifies. No one will know all the situations and answers possible for an emerging market, so make the best calculated guess you can—and move forward. Sometimes, no matter how much research and planning you have done, it feels like you are just 'shooting from the hip.' That's why top management support and clear direction is so critical.

"In all of this, information communications technology is a wonderful tool. As a matter of fact, everyday it is more and more a necessity in order to compete. Technology can help maintain the links between the branches and subsidiaries in Mexico and the parent corporation to help keep those goals and strategies aligned. It can help maintain the critical links between the company and your distributors, and of course, between the company and your customers. However, technology is one tool. Consider your whole organization's structure— the informal as well as the formal structure. Data communications technologies can facilitate business and can even help implement structural change—but it won't cause structural change by itself. Is your company truly global or transnational, or is it structurally multinational at best? Does the company structure support the foreign operations being planned? I remember a gentleman from Westinghouse commenting once that data communications technology will make a good business better, but it will put bad business out of business faster. Don't automate bad systems or generate data without transforming it into information. As I said, data communications technology is a wonderful tool; but it is complementary to and not a replacement for thinking people.

"People are indeed the critical element for your venture's success. I have been very fortunate in having wonderful people to deal with. This is true not only from the corporate view, but also personally. My family has a wonderful attitude about our opportunity. Everyday we get new surprises of some sort, but we all view them as wonderful chances to expand our learning. My children now fluently speak two languages; and my daughter is quickly learning Japanese from her friend in school who is also in Mexico with her family on temporary assignment to a venture in Mexico. Those experiences will stay with my kids forever—no matter what they do in life.

"But not everyone is so fortunate in having an adventurous family. Carlsbad Equipment Corp. does not yet provide whole family cultural training; however, we are looking into it for future ventures and for people coming into our current business. It is important that people have an opportunity to learn about the culture in which they will be emerged in order to avoid culture shock. Culture shock is one of those things that sounds 'fuzzy'—those things that particularly U.S. business execs assume either can't happen to them or that it is something they should be able to get over. Be assured—it can happen, and it can be seriously devastating. Therefore, carefully consider the people you send to the new venture, especially in emerging markets and developing countries. Check the person's cultural sensitivity and international experience, certainly. However, don't overlook absolute personality traits. Sometimes, the people who are the most successful in one culture, fail in another because they rely only on what brought success in the past. They don't know how to find what will succeed in the new environment, and not wanting to look foolish, they may fail before asking for help.

"If you are the person about to start a new venture in Mexico, remember to consciously seek to understand the deep-seated core values and culture that is manifested in the customs you observe. Mexico has a rich history in which many different, well-established cultures and value systems were melded. It is fascinating to learn more and more about them, even though the best we can expect is to be as a distant cousin—empathetic, but not in the immediate family. Don't judge what you learn; just accept the knowledge and strive for understanding.

"Also, don't ignore the obvious. For instance, the U.S. doesn't have as formal a caste system as Mexico, and women in U.S. business have made significant inroads in the past 15 years. We can argue that we need more improvement in both areas; but the point here is that both of these issues are still practices in Mexico. There is a stringent caste system that determines who gets what opportunity; and women in business are almost non-existent except as secretaries and administrators. These things are slowly changing as more young people are moving into business, and more and more are gaining their education abroad. Nevertheless, the old system is still in place. Working through these issues to keep in alignment with your company policies will be challenging. It is fine to be a 'change agent'; however, to be effective you must be cognizant of what is being changed. Don't try to ignore the situation. Take a conscious stand.

"That leads to the point of always conducting your business with integrity. Of course, it seems to be an obvious position—to maintain integrity; however, daily questions arise that appear innocent enough, yet somehow challenge the integrity of you and your company. Something that is regulated by law in the U.S. may not be a legal issue in Mexico, and it seems as if everyone there does it. Or an opportunity may arise that seems to be good for the company and OK for everyone else as well—just perhaps not great for them—for example, donating obsolete equipment to a school to empty the stock and get a tax break at the same time. Is it a question of integrity? Maybe—after all, the people in the school know the stuff is obsolete and why you are making the donation. Does it help them? Maybe—but not as much as if they had a chance to learn on new equipment. Put yourself in their place. How would you feel if your children attended that school? The point is, avoid trying to establish a double set of rules. Consistently maintain the policies your company upholds in the U.S. and your reputation as being a company that operates with integrity will spread a long way.

"If you are going, learn the language. I can't emphasize that enough. The Mexican people are proud of their country and their culture, and with that goes their language. They appreciate your trying to learn and will go out of their way to help you. Don't miss the opportunity. Ha Ha, not to mention, it is a lot easier to get around when you can read the signs.

"Beyond this, I could tell you what I have learned of the Mexican culture and customs. Many things you already know, I suspect. For instance, the Mexican family includes a much broader group of relation than the typical U.S. person thinks of. Although we may refer to 'family' as including cousins, second cousins, etc. we seldom consider them in everyday actions. In Mexico, the whole family is very important to each member, and they will go out of their way to help each other. Business often revolves around family members, and calendars are established around family events. Vacation time spent with the family is precious and cannot be sacrificed. So, understand and expect that the family is important to a Mexican businessman.

"I can tell you that relationships are important, and that business operates more on who knows whom. I can tell you to expect a high degree of formality in business encounters. You will know a Mexican businessman a long time before he will invite you to call him by his first name.

"I can tell you many other things; but, for one thing we are running out of time this evening. Even if we were not, however, I would stop at this point, and ask that you do not take my observations of the Mexican culture and customs as absolute scientific fact. Please do not stereotype the Mexican people. They are a warm and friendly people; and just as everywhere else, each individual is unique in personality and style. The fun is getting to know each person for all the qualities that person has. Please be sensitive to the values and culture of the Mexican people. You will come to value them as much as I do, I'm sure.

Thank you. Good-night"

Interview Questionnaire

GENERAL

1. Is there a general feeling of trust or distrust between
   Mexican employees and Mexican supervisors?
   Mexican employees and U.S. supervisors?
   Mexican business peers and U.S. business peers?
   Mexican competitors and other Mexican companies?
   Mexican competitors and U.S. companies?

2. Is there a difference regarding "sense of community" as
   compared with U.S. groups?
   Among Mexican employees?
   Among Mexican and U.S. employees?
   Among Mexican businessmen?
   Among Mexican competitors?

3. Have you had to behave differently in terms of exercising
   authority than with a U.S. group
   with Mexican customers?
   with Mexican employees?
   with Mexican managers?
   In what ways?

4. Is there a noticeable difference between Mexican and
   Americans in the willingness or the means of expressing
   individual's opinions?
   about business decisions?
   about fellow employees?
   about general political or world situations?

5. Any particular ideas for—managing, selling, servicing, etc.—
   that met with major resistance?
   from customers?
   from employees?
   What was the resistance?

CUSTOMERS & DISTRIBUTORS

6. Are the expectation of Mexican customers different than
   American customers?
   regarding service after sale?
   regarding warranty?
   regarding documentation?
   in other areas?

7. Do you notice different negotiating styles or techniques in
   general in Mexican customers than practiced in the U.S.? In
   what ways?

8. Do you notice different expectations of status & demeanor
   among levels in Mexican customer organization than other
   countries—especially the U.S.? In what ways?

9. Have you seen a ready acceptance of information
   communications technologies among customers? Is acceptance
   or resistance different than what you have experienced in the
   U.S.? In what ways?

10. Is the technology used in the same manner in Mexican
    companies as in U.S. companies? Examples?

11. What criteria do you use to select Mexican distributors?

12. Is the criteria different than what is used to select U.S.
    distributors? In what way?

13. Do you have any unique arrangements required for Mexican
    distributors?
    i.e. Financing, Training, Support, etc.

14. Are all business details contracted or is there more hand-shake
    agreeing between vendor and customers?
    between manufacturers and distributors?

15. Are there major differences between Mexico and the U.S. in how a product is promoted?
    In advertising?
    In marketing promotions?
    In trade shows?
    In other ways?

16. Are there general differences in the contractual arrangements with distributors in Mexico as compared to U.S. distributors?
    with customers in Mexico as compared to U.S. customers?

17. Is the margin structure different with Mexican distributors than U.S. distributors? In what ways?

EMPLOYEES

18. Is there a difference in effectiveness of incentive programs implemented in Mexico than in the U.S.?
    What works?
    What doesn't?
    Why?

19. Is there a noticeable difference in the aspirations of Mexican employees and U.S. employees?
    In what ways?

20. Is there a greater or lesser tendency to establish rules and processes in Mexican groups than American groups?
    Examples:

21. Do Mexican employees prefer to figure out what tasks to do or to be told specifically by a superior?
    Is there a difference in this tendency across genders?
    Across age groups?
    Across education groups?

22. Is there a tendency for long or short term planning among the Mexican managers?
    Is it different than among U.S. managers?

23. Compare the voluntary turnover rates as significantly higher or lower in the Mexican or U.S. sites.
    To what would you attribute the difference?
    What is the "firing" policy in the Mexican site?

Is this different than in the U.S.? In what ways?

24. Is there a difference in selecting a new manager in a Mexican or U.S. site? What are the differences?
    Is there more or less tendency to promote from within in Mexico?

25. Is there a readiness or reluctance to adapt new information communications technologies?
    among Mexican employees?
    among Mexican managers?
    Is this different across age groups? In what ways?
    across genders? In what ways?

26. Have you tried some of the newer management theories, i.e. flex time, self-directed teams, cross functional work areas, etc.? What has been the reaction of the employees?

References

Bartlett, C.A. and Ghoshal, S; *Managing Across Borders;* Harvard Business School Press, MA. 1989.

Bergsten, C.F.; "The World Economy After the Cold War"; *The Commonwealth*, LXXXV, No. 49, Dec. 9, 1991.

Bessen, Jim; "Riding the marketing Information Wave"; *Harvard Business Review* , Sept./Oct., 1993; p. 150.

"Brazil Curbs Tobacco Ads"; Wall Street Journal, January 5, 1995; p. A10.

Cateora, Philip; *International Marketing, Seventh Edition*, Irwin Press; 1990.

Cisneros, Jose Javier Vega; "Mexico espera la regularizacion"; *TelePress Latinoamerica*, No. 24, January/February, 1995; p. 24.

Czinkota, Michael R., Ronkainen, Ilkka A. ; *International Marketing, Second Edition;* The Dryden Press, 1990.

DeGeorge, Richard T.; *Competing with Integrity in International Business*; Oxford University Press; New York & Oxford; 1993.

Economist Intelligence Unit; *The Economist* , February 25th, 1995; p. 11.

Flores, Javier; "The Computers and Peripherals market in Mexico"; American Embassy- Mexico City, Department of Commerce—International Trade Administration; July 1994.

Fosler, Gail D.; *North American Outlook: 1995-1996*; The Conference Board, Inc.; New York, New York; 1995.

Hall, Edward T.; *Beyond Culture;* Doubleday, Anchor Books; New York, New York; Originally published, 1976; Current edition, 1981.

Hall, Edward T.; *The Hidden Dimension*; Doubleday, New York, New York; 1966 (reprinted, 1982).

Hall, Edward T.; *The Silent Language*; Doubleday, Anchor Book edition; New York, New York; original—1959, Anchor Books editions: 1973, 1990.

Hamel, G., & Prahalad, C.K.; "Do You Really Have a Global Strategy?"; *Harvard Business Review*, July-August, 1985.

Hofstede, Geert; *Culture's Consequences—International Differences in Work-Related Values, Vol. 5*; Sage Publications, England & California; 1984.

Hulbert, James M.; *Marketing: A Strategic Perspective*; Impact Publishing Company, New York; 1985.

Ives B., & Jarvenpaa S.; "Competing with Information: Empowering Knowledge Networks with Information Technology"; *1993 Annual Review*, Institute for Information Studies.

Ives B., & Jarvenpaa S.; "Wiring the Stateless Corporation: Empowering the Drivers and Overcoming the Barriers"; *INSIGHT* for SIM.

Kuczmarski, Thomas D.; *Managing New Products*; Prentice Hall; New Jersey; 1988.

Levitt, T.; "The Globalization of Markets"; *Harvard Business Review:*; Going Global-Succeeding in World Markets. (originally in HBR, May-June, 1983.)

Markus, M. Lynne; Keil, Mark; "If We Build It, They Will Come: Designing Information Systems That People Want to Use"; *Sloan Management Review* , Summer, 1994; p. 11.

Marsh, J. and Vanston, L.; *Interactive Multimedia and Telecommunications;* Technology Futures Inc.; Austin, TX.; 1992.

Mott, et. al..; *The Arthur Andersen North American Business Source Book;* Triumph Books, Chicago; 1994.

Nolan, Richard L; Haeckel, Stephan, H.: "Managing by Wire"; *Harvard Business Review*, Sept./Oct., 1993; p. 122.

O'Toole, James; *Four Poles of the Good Society; An Executive Guide to the Timeless Ideas that Shape Today's World*; whitepaper, 1993.

Perry, M.; "In a Global Market, the Challenges Never End"; Corporate Strategies for Global Competitive Advantage; The Conference Board: Report Number 996.

Pine II, Joseph B.; Peppers; Don, Rogers, Martha: "Do You Want to Keep Your Customers Forever?"; *Harvard Business Review*, March/April, 1995.

Pine II, Joseph B.; Victor, Bart; Boynton, Andrew C.: "Making Mass Customization Work"; *Harvard Business Review,* Sept./Oct., 1993; p. 108.

Porter, Michael E.; *The Competitive Advantage of Nations*; The Free Press, New York; 1990.

Pyramid Research, Inc.; *Telecom Markets in Mexico*; Cambridge, MA; 1994.

Roy, Amitava Dutta; "America Latina Se "Internetiza""; *TelePress Latinoamerica*; No. 24, January/February, 1995; p.21-22.

Roy, Amitava Dutta; "El mundo financiero y la Internet"; *TelePress Latinoamerica,* No. 24, January/February, 1995; p. 24.

Sesit, M.; "Flocking to the Frontier;", Wall Street Journal, Sept. 21, 1993.

Slywotzky, A., & Shapiro, B.; "Leveraging to Beat the Odds: The New Marketing Mind-Set"; *Harvard Business Review*; Vol. 71, Number 5, Sept.-Oct. 1993.

Stone, N.; "The Globalization of Europe: An Interview with Wisse Dekker"; Going Global-Succeeding in World Markets; *Harvard Business Review.* (originally printed in HBR, May-June 1989).

The Economist; *Guide to Global Economic Indicators*; The Economist Books, Ltd.; John Wiley & Sons, Inc.; 1994.

Thurburn, Lee; *Mexico: The New "Land of Opportunity" , A Guide to Doing Business In Mexico*; PMA Press, Ft. Worth, Texas; 1993.

Urban, Glen L., Hauser, John R.; *Design and Marketing of New Products*; Prentice Hall; New Jersey; 1980.

U.S. Department of Commerce; *A Basic Guide To Exporting*; January 1992.

U.S. Department of Commerce; "Labor in Mexico—A guide to Mexican Compensation and Labor Law"; NAFTA Facts, #8502, 1995.

U.S. Department of Commerce; "Maquiladoras and the NAFTA"; NAFTA Facts Mexico, #3008, 1995.

Webster's Unified Dictionary and Encyclopedia; H.S. Stuttman Co. Inc., New York, N.Y.; 1959.

Index